Paul for a New Day

PAUL
for a
New Day

ROBIN SCROGGS

FORTRESS PRESS
Philadelphia

Library of Congress Catalog Card Number 76–9719
ISBN 0–8006–1242–6

5784176   Printed in U.S.A.   1–1242

Contents

for Mother

Preface

This book is not intended to be a balanced statement spoken with moderation. Nor does it even begin to discuss all aspects of Paul's thinking. The beginning student of Paul can and should find other books which are more comprehensive and inclusive. What I have attempted to do is to seek out that deepest heart of the Apostle's understanding of Christian existence and to press that understanding to the limit of my powers. It is not intended to be a book that can be read without challenge to the reader. I have spent too many unsettling years with Paul's thinking to believe that an accurate reading of him can take place without an agonizing and surprisingly joyous reappraisal of the self. For me this agony is an ongoing process, but it has been the most fruitful agony of my life. It hardly sounds nice for an author to wish distress upon his readers. If after reading this book, however, there is neither joy nor uneasiness, either the reader has not read perceptively, or I have not written clearly, or perhaps both.

Paul is too often seen by the popular mind as an abstract, mythological theologian who says too much about the future and not enough about the present. Even within professional exegetical circles, the emphasis is usually laid upon hope for salvation in the future. This book stresses the other side. Without denying the importance of the future and without simplistically assuming that all is right in the church, it attempts to emphasize and celebrate the affirmations Paul makes about the believer's life in the *present* as fulfillment of God's original intent in creation. Salvation is thus not a future escape from human existence; it is the (partly realized) present result of the liberating power from God which transforms persons *into* authentic human beings.

As such, this transformed human existence is properly called "eschatological." The word denotes the ultimate and final reality of God's dealings with persons. It is frequently given a temporal "location," namely, in the future. In this sense the term *eschatological* points to life in heaven in the kingdom of God. But it is properly used *wherever* and *whenever* God chooses to cause that ultimate reality to come into existence. Since Paul understands that act of God to be taking place *now* wherever people in community live under justification by grace, it is appropriate to use the term, as I do in this book, to point to present Christian being and doing.

The material for this book was originally delivered as lectures at a retreat for ministers of the Colorado Conference of the United Church of Christ. Those days were, for me, a stimulating and refreshing time for both mind and body, and I wish here to acknowledge my gratitude to the participants for the lively and warm discussions that emerged. An incident from that conference, however, will perhaps illuminate both the movement of the pages which follow and something of the resistance that contemporary Americans instinctively have against Paul. The opening lecture was essentially chapter 1 of this book, which deals with the new existence, or new being, brought into reality by God's act of justification. And, as in the present format, I wished to reserve *any* talk about ethical action until the last lecture. After the first lecture was over I was immediately bombarded by a number of very serious questioners, and all questions had something to do with action. "But you didn't tell us what to do!" After several such questions were put on the table, I stopped them and said something like, "Do you realize that all your questions so far have to do with ethics, which was not the subject of tonight's discussion? Tonight's lecture had to do with being, not doing." A very perceptive minister then replied, "Well, after two hundred years of American pragmatism, what do you expect?" What, indeed!

My interpretation of Paul is rooted in that classical stream of Augustine, Luther, and Rudolf Bultmann, although I depart from them at decisive points. The reader will not find other points of view represented. Professional scholars will know how much scholarly discussion has been eliminated because of the nature of the book. I hope they will be sympathetic to the necessity of such omissions, which would be inexcusable in a technical volume.

What the reader *will* find is an attempt to enlist the support of some modern, nontheological models from the realms of psychology and sociology, which will, hopefully, lead to a more exciting and illuminating understanding for modern persons of what Paul is about. In a book of this scope it is impossible adequately to describe or defend my use of such models. In the future I hope to produce a substantial volume which will validate my appropriation of these nontheological methodologies, an appropriation which in the present volume will simply have to be evaluated on the basis of whatever light it sheds for the reader on the text.

I do, however, at least wish to raise the question about the legitimacy of such appropriation in theology and to make a preliminary statement. Theology, usually at least, is based on the acceptance of a transcendent reality called God. Christian theology celebrates the activity of this transcendent reality in the person of Jesus Christ. Psychoanalytic and sociological sciences, while logically neutral over the question of God, pursue their activity as a completely human science, that is, without needing to deal with the relation of this human reality to the transcendent. Thus, theology and such sciences *can* go their own separate ways without any necessary conflict. But if someone brings them together as I am suggesting, if someone proposes that psychoanalytic theory, for example, can indeed describe human transformation, which theology calls "salvation," thus seeming to reduce God's act to some immanent human process—then it is at this point that the issue becomes crucial. Am I in danger of pushing a "reductionist" theology in which the transcendent reality is in effect eliminated?

I would like to respond to this with two points. The first point has to do with what Christian theology is talking about— that is, what it says God is concerned with; what *is* the intent of the act or acts of God? I believe the proper answer to this question (although I know there are others) is that God's acts aim at the creation of an authentic human community. In classical language, God is trying to "save" humanity, and this salvation, while in many systems it is seen as primarily future, eternal life in the kingdom of God, is not limited by *most* systems entirely to the future. There is legitimacy, therefore, in speaking of salvation as a present reality in persons and communities who are living in obedience and love toward God. My researches into formative Christianity have convinced me that Jesus, the earliest church in general, Paul, the author of the Gospel of John, and others, not only *could* speak of salvation as a present reality, but they in fact stressed it, although without eliminating its ultimate futurity. And salvation as a present phenomenon has to do with authentic human existence, true creaturely life, or whatever similar term one chooses to use. Thus I believe it is theologically legitimate to reflect upon any attempt to describe what that existence would look like and how it would be achieved.

Secondly, to appropriate secular theory is not to imply that social science can do God's work for him. *To describe something is not in and of itself to provide the power to realize that something into existence.* Thus in no way am I proposing to reduce the power of God's act in Christ to human reflection and willing. One could even say that for all the accuracy of any secular description of authentic humanity, *only* the act of God *in Christ* can bring that humanity into existence. It seems to me that such an extreme statement borders on theological imperialism, and I could not myself make that affirmation. It seems to me more in keeping with our noetic finitude to put it this way: the believer celebrates the transformation of persons through the power of God's act in Christ, rejoices in the deeper understanding of that transformation afforded him or her by whatever source of knowledge, and remains open to the possibility that God may work his transformations apart from the church and explicit Christian statements about ultimate reality.

It is a pleasure to offer thanks to my secretary Carol Eck and to my typist Cajsa Elo for their careful work with various stages of the manuscript. Special thanks go to Marilee, my wife, for her honest and insightful critique of my reflections as well as for nourishment of my life as a whole. To numbers of my colleagues and student-friends at Chicago Theological Seminary I owe the gift of a sharing and caring community, without which I would not have come to understand Paul as I now do. They have helped me experience the reality to which Paul's words point.

June, 1976

> . . . it was all
> Shining, it was Adam and maiden,
>   The sky gathered again
> And the sun grew round that very day.
>
> Dylan Thomas, "Fern Hill"

1

Justification:
Eschatological Creation

The trouble with Paul is that he has too many friends and too many enemies. The one thing that the friends and enemies tend to have in common is that they do not really know what Paul is all about. At least the Paul I hear defended and the Paul I hear attacked is not the Paul that I have come to know and appreciate. The purpose of this book is to share with you the Paul I know; perhaps, hopefully, by the end you will have gained a new friend for yourselves.

The difficulties in understanding this figure are, however, immense, and it is no surprise to encounter the distortions that one does. Paul's own letters suggest that he was not always understood even by the people he was writing to, people who in almost all instances had known him personally and had heard him speak many times. How much more likely are we, at a remove of nineteen hundred years, to have problems!

There seem to me to be three really significant obstacles. The first is that Paul's theology is a mythological system—if you will permit a very specific definition of mythology which stems from Rudolf Bultmann, namely, that myth is the narration of the transcendent erupting into the immanent, the invading of the ordinary course of historical causality by divine power.[1] Myth is thus not simply a story about gods, nor is it pejoratively to be equated with an untrue, false, or humanly irrelevant reality.

1. Rudolf Bultmann, *Jesus Christ and Mythology* (New York: Charles Scribner's Sons, 1958), pp. 14–18.

1

Paul's myth is that in Christ God has acted to judge and save humanity, opening up the possibility of resurrection existence in the kingdom of God. The preexistence of Christ, incarnation, resurrection, and second coming are part of his vocabulary. For persons who have accepted the world view of modern science, this language is impossible and obscurantist.

Of course, in our days of "The Exorcist," science fiction, and Hobbits, it is apparent that for many people the rejection of Paul because his theology is mythological is simply an excuse. People need, and do respond to, mythological systems. On the other side of the argument, consider how most people ignore the warnings of ecological doom from the scientists themselves. The conclusion is, I think, inescapable: people listen to the science they want to listen to; they listen to the mythology they want to listen to. Nevertheless, Paul's mythology *is* an obstacle, even if partly a contrived one. Matters are not made easier by the fact that his mythology is from a culture far removed from our own.

For all the difficulties which emerge with Paul's sometimes opaque mythology, however, it remains for many of us a *familiar* mythology. And this is the second major obstacle. We throw off terms like *justification* and *grace* without understanding either their historical or existential meanings. Paul has been domesticized in the household of faith, and we make him a comfortable companion by no longer really listening to him. After all, we've heard it all before. It would almost be easier for us if we could start over from scratch. At least then there might be some wonder in our response to what he has to say.

This domestication is not a new means by which to contain the torrents of the Apostle. That had its beginning in the early church, perhaps even before Paul was dead. We catch our first real glimpses of it in the deutero-Pauline letters, especially the Pastorals.[2] These letters can best be seen as attempts by some

2. It is crucial for the nonspecialist to know that scholars have for many years recognized that not all of the books in the New Testament attributed to Paul were actually written by him. Several, it is nearly universally acknowledged, were written at a time after Paul's death by unknown authors who wrote in his name. No doubt for these authors Paul was a hero, but it is equally clear that they chose not to go the radical way of the historical Apostle. Scholars call these later books "deutero-Pauline" writings; they include Ephesians, Colossians, 1 and 2 Timothy, Titus, and probably 2 Thessalonians. There is considerable doubt about 2 Thessalonians and some

theologians to create a Paul safe for the establishment or main-
line church.   In these letters "Paul" gives sage and safe counsel,
while the craggy reality of the historical Apostle almost never
surfaces.   And let us not be too quick to explain away this distortion of Paul by saying that these writers just didn't really understand him.   It is, it seems to me, more likely that they understood
him all too well, and didn't like what they understood!

Behind both of these obstacles, we have hinted, lurks something deeper and more sinister so that there may be a third,
really basic obstacle behind both of the other two.   And this I
think is the case.   I am becoming increasingly convinced that the
basic reality behind the avoidance and miscomprehension of
Paul is *fear*.   For I believe that Paul has always been a dangerous radical for the establishment church.   He has proven too hot
to handle, too searing to take straight, too threatening to our life
of ease in Zion.   It may thus be possible that the misunderstand-
ing is somehow a deliberate one, intended to distance or domes-
ticize a thinker who calls so many of our pious values into question, a thinker who would jar us loose from all the supports and
crutches which are absolutely essential to us if we would continue to live in our same undisturbed way.   Our lives may not
all be filled with peace and joy, but at least we wear them like
comfortable old clothes which we hate to throw away.

If this is so, then my task, while difficult, is clear.   It is to make
it impossible for us any longer to ignore the radical challenge of
the Apostle.   It is to tear down the facade of the domesticated
Paul so that the real Paul can confront us, assault us, if you will,
with his challenge.   I am not proposing to engage in guerrilla
theatre.   The prospect is rather one of joy and happiness, however scary.   But I challenge you to open yourselves to existential
involvement at every turn.

It is my confident belief that Paul is not peddling an abstract,
mythological ideology.   His language is, of course, mythological;
it is, in fact, his everyday speech.   Through this language, however, shines a vision of the tragedy of humanity and a profound

---

about Colossians.   For a helpful introduction to the questions of authorship
the reader should consult the relevant sections in Norman Perrin, *The New
Testament: An Introduction* (New York: Harcourt Brace Jovanovitch, 1974).

understanding of how God's gracious act in Christ really does
free people to choose to leave that tragedy and to live as people in
a world remolded to the image of God.[3]

Paul's theology can stand on its own. But I confess that part
of my confidence in Paul stems from the fact that I see significant
correlations between his vision and that of an interpretation of
human existence by a certain movement in psychoanalytic theory. This approach, best exemplified by Norman O. Brown,
bases itself upon Freud's application of his clinically based theories of the individual psyche to society as a whole.[4] Now I am
well aware that Freud is not especially au courant in many circles
today. I can only say that Brown's analysis of the human dilemma is to me convincing and that there is a startling correspondence between Brown's description of what would have to
happen if people were to escape this dilemma and Paul's own
statement of what, in fact, has happened through Christ in the
Christian communities. There will be no space here adequately
to describe Brown's complex interpretation of Freud or even to
show just how the correspondences work out. Where possible, I
will give the germ of the argument, so that one can get at least a
glimpse of how I see it helping us better to understand the deepest reality Paul is trying to describe.

One final presupposition. Scholars have reached no consensus
about how to interpret Paul; several classical interpretations
have maintained themselves over the years and are not likely to
die. It is my conviction that Augustine and Luther were correct
at least in finding the heart of Paul's thought in the cluster of
motifs summed up in the phrase "justification by grace through

3. It is my conviction, one I share with many scholars and theologians, that
much of Paul's mythological vocabulary is best understood in a nonliteral
sense. This in no way deprives it of meaning, nor does it any the less point
to actual, divine realities. Rather it *frees* the language from abstraction to
point to the concrete, divine redeeming activity among people. The term
demythologization is frequently used to point to this mode of understanding
mythological language. Such a term is appropriate, but it does not necessarily
mean that the language should be discarded. It does suggest that we should
know what it means when we use such language.

4. Norman O. Brown, *Life Against Death* (Middletown, Ct.: Wesleyan Uni-
versity Press, 1959) and *Love's Body* (New York: Random House, 1966);
Herbert Marcuse, *Eros and Civilization* (New York: Beacon House, 1955).
Among the pertinent works of Sigmund Freud himself, the most suggestive is
Civilization and Its Discontents (New York: W. W. Norton, 1961), as well as
Beyond the Pleasure Principle, trans. James Strachey (New York: Liveright,
1970) and *The Future of an Illusion* (New York: Liveright, 1964).

faith," although neither of them understood all the complexities of the Apostle. It is this cluster which will concern us in these chapters; other motifs, which are undeniably important to Paul, must remain muted or even tacit. Were there opportunity, those other motifs, usually clustered around that of "being in Christ," or the so-called Christ mysticism, could be shown to be consonant with the interpretation of justification which follows.[5]

THE WORLD OF SIN AND DEATH

As we will see shortly, the term *justification* comes out of the context of the law court. Already, then, we are within a situation where some people are accused of acting wrongly. That means, when transferred to a religious situation, "sinning." Thus, justification in the religious context has to do with a situation where people are sinners or are accused of being so. God's act of justification is, in fact, from Paul's perspective, God's way of dealing with sin.[6] Thus, before we can explore what Paul understands God to have done, we must come to terms with Paul's understanding of what persons have done, namely, to sin.

The discussion begins as if it is going to exist on the level of the utterly banal. What does Paul think of sin? Well, to borrow from Coolidge, he is against it. But fortunately Paul has a few surprises for us. In the first place, he considers every person outside of Christ to be constantly a sinner. Now after two thousand years of church tradition in which this has become dogma, we can hardly appreciate the radicalness in his day of this judgment. While I do not believe that Paul invented the notion of original sin, despite the long-standing tradition that says he did, he nevertheless considers sin to be universal.[7] It is not just

5. The informed scholar will be as painfully aware as I am of the immense difficulties seemingly being swept aside by this sentence. The present book, however, is not a proper vehicle to argue the matter. The nonspecialist will find views emphasizing other dimensions of Paul's thought in Albert Schweitzer, *The Mysticism of Paul the Apostle* (New York: Seabury Press, 1955); William D. Davies, *Paul and Rabbinic Judaism: Some Rabbinic Elements in Pauline Theology* (New York: Harper & Row, 1955); and Krister Stendahl, "The Apostle Paul and the Introspective Conscience of the West," *The Writings of St. Paul*, ed. W. Meeks (New York: W. W. Norton, 1972), pp. 422–34.

6. Scholarly debate over the nuances of the meaning of justification still continues. Perhaps still the best introduction to the discussion is in Bultmann, *Theology of the New Testament*, trans. Kendrick Grobel (New York: Charles Scribner's Sons, 1954), 1:270–85.

7. See the arguments in Robin Scroggs, *The Last Adam* (Philadelphia: Fortress Press, 1966), pp. 77–79.

universal in the sense that sooner or later even the most righteous
and pious folk are going to make some slip. No, sin is a matter
of *existence* which permeates the total self in all its realities.
This teaching is not only startling, if we hear it afresh; it is also
potentially offensive. Certainly it was offensive to the pious Jews
and Christians of Paul's day who vigorously opposed his views.
It is just, of course, to point one's finger at the murderer and
rapist; but what sense does it make to point that same finger at a
pious pharisee or ascetic Christian or middle-class American
Protestant? But point his finger Paul might. It forces us to the
awareness that Paul is not speaking of a kind of action but of a
mode of being, a mode which in Paul's mind envelops the righteous pharisee every bit as much as it does the hardened and
callous criminal.[8]

In the second place, we must exclude one way out which has
over and over again been suggested: that Paul opposed the law
because it was too hard to fulfill. Were this so, then perhaps
Paul could legitimately accuse the religious person of a sinful act
here or there. This is, indeed, the stance taken by the author of
the Book of Acts when he has Peter exclaim, "Now therefore why
do you make trial of God by putting a yoke upon the neck of the
disciples which neither our fathers nor we have been able to
bear?" (Acts 15:10). But Paul has no such hesitation. Speaking
of himself, he writes, "If any other man thinks he has reason for
confidence in the flesh, I have more: circumcised on the eighth
day, of the people of Israel, of the tribe of Benjamin, a Hebrew
born of Hebrews; as to the law a Pharisee, as to zeal a persecutor
of the church, as to righteousness under the law blameless" (Phil.
3:4–6). And in another place: "I advanced in Judaism beyond
many of my own age among my people, so extremely zealous was
I for the traditions of my fathers" (Gal. 1:14). The pharisee is
not a sinner when he fails to fulfill the law; somehow he is a
sinner precisely when he *does* fulfill the law.

8. For every interpreter dealing sympathetically with Paul's debate about
justification, there is an extremely difficult semantic problem. Paul is, of
course, arguing against the pharisaic position, as he understands it, but
primarily as it appears in the guise of Jewish *Christians*, who are called
"the Judaizers." Given this situation, it is virtually impossible for a modern
author when writing about Paul *not* to sound as though he or she is attacking
Judaism, even though he or she, like Paul, is really fighting against a position
taken by *Christians*. I trust it will be clear to the reader that I am in no
way attempting to take a stand against the synagogue.

In the third place, Paul has a surprise for us in that we cannot find much foothold in the Pauline letters for the view that says the real sin of the pharisee lay in his self-righteousness, his considering himself to be better than others. We do find this view expressed in the gospel traditions, and it is true that Paul speaks negatively of a kind of boasting which is linked both with the life of Torah obedience and false Christian pride (e.g., Rom. 3:27; 1 Cor. 1.26–31). But the real burden of Paul's argument lies elsewhere, and it should also be kept in mind that rabbinic literature is full of models of humility. If we take this literature seriously, the attitude of the pharisee is more likely to have been anxiety than braggadocio.

There is a fourth and final surprise concerning Paul's view of sin; he drops a couple of tantalizing clues in Romans. In chapter 5 he is setting up the contrast between the human condition and the divine act of grace. He points to this human condition at the beginning of the sentences with structurally similar phrases (participial phrases in the original Greek): "while we were yet helpless" (v. 6); "while we were yet sinners" (v. 8); "while we were enemies" (v. 10). *To be a sinner means to be both helpless and hostile.* Far from the sinner being a violent person of action, Paul speaks of impotence. (The Greek word, translated "helpless," can denote a person's physical frailty or even physical illness.) Being a sinner is equatable with being unable to achieve what it is desirable to achieve. This is startling enough, but the second word, *enemy*, is even more unusual. Enemy to whom? The context makes it clear. "For if while we were enemies we were reconciled to God by the death of his Son, much more, now that we are reconciled, shall we be saved by his life" (v. 10). *The sinner is hostile toward God*, and the act of justification is somehow an act of reconciliation, which removes that hostility. Again we must be careful not to read into Paul ideas which have their origin elsewhere. One medieval theory, or rather distortion thereof, of the atonement did speak of the angry God and the act of Christ as that act which reconciles God toward sinful persons. But for Paul, it is exactly the opposite. Paul never speaks of God being reconciled to persons; reconciliation is always of persons toward God. Mankind seems to be the offended party, not God. He will even plead with the Corinthians, "Be reconciled to God" (2 Cor. 5:20).

Thus the big surprise so far is that while Paul is certainly against sin, he has a view of it which far transcends the usual notions of unrighteous conduct. We can better speak of sinful existence, an existence which contains within it qualities of impotence and hostility toward God *even in the moment of perfect fulfillment of the law.* This may sound mysterious, but we are now not far from discovering the meaning of Paul's vision.

Let me first state it in non-Pauline language. Sin is the total life-project of earning one's salvation. As we will see, the means by which this project is carried on can vary tremendously. For the Jew, especially the pious pharisee, the project was done in terms of bowing in obedience to the law of the Hebrew Bible as interpreted by current exegetes. It is what Paul calls "justification by works," and that which he sets over against justification by grace. And it raises the problem in its greatest paradoxical form. *Precisely in the obedience to the law lies the disobedience before God.* Paul writes passionately, "Brethren, my heart's desire and prayer to God for them [the Jews] is that they may be saved. I bear them witness that they have a zeal for God, but it is not enlightened. For being ignorant of the justification that comes from God, and seeking to establish their own, they were not obedient to God's act of justification" (Rom. 10:1–3). We still have to see precisely what God's act of justification consists of, but for the moment we can remain with the charge against the pharisees, that disobedience consists in the attempt to establish one's own justification—to understand one's life as a project to win and secure one's existence. It is, however subtly, to put God in one's debt, to say to God, "You owe me eternal life."

Even more crucial is the dialogue within the self in such a life-project. By attending to this project I attempt to ease the anxiety about my own security. But as Bultmann has suggested, this anxiety, while it may be repressed, never goes away, and so I can never cease attending to this project.[9] In fact I never do anything else. My total attention is focused on this project, and I *become* the project. Not only is this true for myself; it is also

9. Rudolf Bultmann, "Christ the End of the Law," *Essays: Philosophical and Theological* (New York: Macmillan Publishing Co., 1955), pp. 36–66.

true for that reality I touch outside of myself, particularly other people. Others are useful to me only insofar as they can contribute to my project. Thus I use them and they never cease being only an object by which I attempt to overcome my anxiety (the "I-It" relationship of Buber). I am not able genuinely to relate to them as an independent person. Thus I cannot be to them a neighbor fulfilling their needs. As long as I strive to justify myself, I cannot love.

Already by implication we have left that specific situation of the pious pharisee seeking to win his own existence through obedience to the Torah; but I think this is not only legitimate, it is absolutely necessary if we are to understand the Apostle. Paul himself signaled this movement. In the Corinthian correspondence he speaks of the Greeks seeking wisdom. Again it is Bultmann who has perceptively shown that here Paul is attacking another cultural manifestation of the same attempt to secure one's life.[10] In the case of the Greeks interested in rational systems, the project consists of the construction of a philosophy or theology *by* which the self can be understood, *in* which the self can be placed, and existence secured. Paul rejects this specification of the project just as clearly as he does that of the Jew.

The truth of the matter, it seems to me, is that Paul has uncovered a universal human mode of being. For it is germane to our existence in history that we are anxious about ourselves—again, however subtly and in how completely a repressed manner.[11] Our lives *do* become projects for securing our place in the sun. We *do* use other people as part of this project. I am a teacher and scholar. My project is to teach so that my students will say I'm a good and exciting teacher; to write articles and books so that my scholarly peers will compliment me on my ideas and my writing. I depend enormously on community response to me. Thus I have to live my life—at least I have to put up the proper appearances—so that the community will say I'm a good person. I am sensitive to criticism; real or imagined, it doesn't matter. And the quantitative adding up of compliments in a row doesn't make the next criticism any less stinging. Nor does

10. Bultmann, *Theology*, vol. 1, pp. 240–41.
11. The inevitable and crucial dimension of the subconscious seems to me not adequately taken into account by Stendahl in his article cited in note 5, above.

it matter whether what I use to secure my selfhood is big or small, important or trivial. One's tennis skill, bowling score, grade record, armchair quarterbacking ability, physical appearance, tastefulness in clothes—all these are equally grist for the mill of the project. All this as a total package is what Paul is attacking when he attacks the process of justification by works.

If we are really to understand him, we must also see to what extent our own middle-class Protestant work ethic (to which Catholics have also succumbed) is solidly grounded in the project of justification by works. We live our lives by what Marcuse calls the "performance principle." Everything depends on how we perform, and we are rewarded on the basis of that performance. That the life of the church today is also infected by the idea of justification by works surely needs no comment. Can it possibly be that we are as enmeshed in the culture of sin and death as were the pharisees?

For this culture Paul attacks is not only a culture of sin, but one of death as well. Indeed, Paul cannot separate the two. Sin brings death, both in the future and somehow in the present as well. One may be physically alive yet really be living in death. This close connection between sin and death emerges clearly in a text which is extremely difficult but which we cannot disregard:

> What then shall we say? That the law is sin? By no means! Yet, if it had not been for the law, I should not have known sin. I should not have known what it is to covet if the law had not said, "You shall not covet." But sin, finding opportunity in the commandment, wrought in me all kinds of covetousness. Apart from the law sin lies dead. I was once alive apart from the law, but when the commandment came, sin revived and I died; the very commandment which promised life proved to be death to me. For sin, finding opportunity in the commandment, deceived me and by it killed me. So the law is holy, and the commandment is holy and just and good. [Rom. 7:7–12]

Paul is here dealing with the question raised during his life and ever since by pious folk, both Jews and Christians. Why shouldn't I obey the law? Why shouldn't I act ethically? Are you suggesting that we are free to eat, drink, and be merry, and kick our brother in the teeth? You are talking as if the law is sin itself, and that is rubbish!

Paul here and elsewhere agrees in part with his detractors.

The law is not sin; it is holy, just, and good. Nevertheless, and this is where all the emphasis lies, there is something in law, in rules, which by standing over me as an *ought*, "thou shalt not . . . ," destroys me, *even if I am obedient to the commandment.* The commandment promises life but effects death instead.

But what is this commandment? I think it is neither an accident nor simply as one possible illustration from among a number that the Apostle cites the commandment against covetousness. The result of the process is that one's existence is qualified by "all kinds of covetousness"—a phrase which is pointing, I believe, to the basic description of the attempt to justify oneself in the law. Life under law is a life of *total covetousness*. And covetousness is death. "Sin revived and I died." We must not forget that the context of this passage is the attack upon the righteous pharisee, who is a sinner even as he fulfills the commandment. It is this life which Paul says is qualified by all covetousness. But how can this be?[12]

At this point, where Paul gets especially difficult, I believe we can find help in Freud's theory about the development of the superego. In fact, with this as a model, we can then turn to answer the baffling question we have raised about Paul's understanding of the human tragedy. I can, of course, only speak of the specific parts of Freud's theory which pertain to the issue, and even these in only the sketchiest manner.

You will recall that the child suffers in the oedipal stage with great anxiety and ambivalence toward the parents. The male child, for example, has desire for the mother and fear of the father.[13] The fear is that the father will kill (castrate) the child. The child develops aggressive feelings toward the father. At a certain point the tension becomes too great to continue. While the history of female development is different, the *result*

12. Many readers may think these comments questionable in the light of what immediately follows in Romans 7, namely the inner debate within the self described in vv. 13–25. These are among the most difficult in all of Paul's correspondence, and it is impossible to deal with them here. It must suffice to say that most scholars take that passage to refer to Paul's *Christian* interpretation of what *pre*-Christian life was really like, not a self-awareness of the person while in that pre-Christian existence. That is, the tension described was an unconscious reality, and the passage intends to say nothing about the ability to fulfill the commandments.

13. For a convenient summary by Freud himself of this complex development, see Sigmund Freud. *The Ego and the Id*, ed. James Strachey and trans. Joan Riviere (New York: W. W. Norton, 1974), pp. 18–29.

is essentially the same. The resolution to the crisis represses the desire and introjects into the self the image of the parents (identification), while at the same time turning the aggression inward against the self. The collusion of the parent-image and the inward-turned aggression creates the superego, that part of the psyche which Freud in his later life saw increasingly as a demonic, despotic, unrealistic power.[14] This resolution creates the conscience (although the superego is not to be equated simply with the conscience—the superego is largely unconscious, while the conscience is only the conscious part of it). The child learns to become obedient to avoid punishment. To be disobedient, to sin, might bring death.

Here emerges the same association of sin and death that Paul and the Judaism of his day so clearly state. If one disobeys God, he or she dies. Now Freud argued long ago that the Jewish God is a cosmic projection of the image of the father.[15] I believe this to be correct, at the same time insisting that this says nothing about the existence or nonexistence of God. It says something rather about how God is *understood*. If this be so, then Freud's insight helps us to understand the Jewish image of God as Father, and thus helps us see what Paul is striving to say. Before we are through, however, we will see that Paul is in effect showing that this Jewish image is incorrect. He redefines the Father.

Furthermore, it is crucial to remember that the superego "contains" the aggression, now directed inwardly in part, but also unconsciously still turned against the parent. Paul, I think, is aware of this reality as it was expressed in the life of the pious Jew engaged in the attempt to justify himself before God his Father. You will remember that Paul says sinful existence is *hostile* toward God, and that the result of the act of God in Christ is a reconciliation with the Father, the resolution of the hostility.

Now it is possible to understand why Paul picks the command against covetousness as the summary of the law.[16] Covetousness

14. See Sigmund Freud, *Civilization and Its Discontents* (New York: W. W. Norton, 1961), pp. 70–80.
15. Freud seems to think this of all religions with male deities. See *The Future of an Illusion*, pp. 23–28. He dealt with Judaism specifically in *Moses and Monotheism*, trans. Katherine Jones (New York: Vintage, 1955).
16. So also S. Lyonnet, "L'Histoire du salut selon le chapitre VII de I'Epitre aux Romains," *Biblica* 43 (1962):144–47.

is a primary expression of aggression—the attempt to possess, control, seize from another, and, metaphorically at least, to kill. To be obedient to the Torah in an attempt to justify oneself by works covertly expresses that primal hostility and aggression against God the Father. Aggression is the reaction against the authoritative, awesome Father, who says, "Thou shalt not . . . ," thus putting an end to freedom. The obvious act of rebellion is, of course, to defy the commandment. Equally, however, if with far greater subtlety, aggression is expressed in the response, "Well, I'll jolly well do it all by myself." It is the covetous attempt to seize the power of life from God himself; in effect, it is an attempt to kill God.

The Jewish author Richard Rubenstein expresses this relationship beautifully. Writing about himself in explicit relation to the Pauline passages about covetousness, he says, "Every attempt I made to comply with the Law, thereby subordinating myself to God, contained an incitement to rebel against him." There is, in fact, a "peculiar mixture of rebelliousness and submissiveness involved in the act of obedience."[17] Here reverberates both the impotence and the aggression Paul has spoken of in Romans 5. This recalls also to mind that famous story about Luther, as he struggled with his understanding of God. As he strove to become perfect, to fulfill all the laws as he understood them, his superior kindly counseled him to think more of God's love and his own love of God. To this Luther is said to have replied, "I don't love God; I hate him."

One final point. For the pious Jew, true life, eternal life, was a future reality. A stock rabbinic phrase ran, "This life is but a vestibule for the world to come." True life is thus a *postponed* reality, not something in present existence. What exists now is the need to be obedient to the Father so that in the last judgment one may pass through into that eternal life. This is a correlate to Freud's theory about the inevitable renunciation of the striving for present pleasure by the child, as it begins to learn the stern lessons of the reality principle. In Jewish apocalyptic thought, just as for Freud, the pleasure principle (life now) is

17. Richard L. Rubenstein, *My Brother Paul* (New York: Harper & Row, 1972), p. 11.

replaced by the reality principle with its promise of future re-
ward (life in heaven). We might call this the "postponement
principle," which can then take its place alongside the "performance principle."

Permit me to sum up all of these various strands. Paul reveals
that he has a profound sense for the tragedy of the human project. It has its roots in mankind's anxiety about itself, resulting
in the attempt to secure the self by works of whatever sort. Instead of finding that security, however, the self lives a life, or
rather lives a death, of impotence, hostility, and aggression toward both God and persons. Thus the project inevitably ends in
failure. Life is always a postponed future, and therefore is always never.

I have devoted so much space to Paul's understanding of sin
because I am concerned at the very beginning to show that his
theology is not an abstraction from real life or simply a culture-
and timebound mythology, but rather is a description of the
roots of human existence that can speak to us in our own anxiety
and pride, as individuals and as churches in our own times. But
it is now time to turn to the motif of justification by grace. And
again my ultimate aim is to show that the Apostle's description is
a very real and comprehensible response to his understanding of
the human tragedy.

JUSTIFICATION BY GRACE

First we must set the term *justification* in its proper context.
It is legal language, taken from ancient Israel's law courts. The
proper, technical translation should be *acquittal*. It denotes the
act of the judge toward the accused which declares him or her
innocent. It is thus an act of restoration, returning the person to
full acceptance within the community. To justify is to put in
the right, or to "right-wise." The opposite of "to justify" is thus
"to condemn." The judge in ancient Israel, however, was not
merely a neutral party, deciding the merits of a case brought
before him by someone else. The judge was at times an active
partner, seeking out the injured and bringing the guilty to trial.
Thus sometimes "to justify" has the nuance of "to vindicate."

Since in Israel God is the judge par excellence, the term *justifi-*

cation soon is theologized. God is the judge of Israel and justifies or condemns his people for their righteousness or sin. In
early times this act of judgment was apparently associated with
the New Year's festival and was thus a repeated event. In the
final transformation of the term, God's act of judgment is pushed
into the future and becomes a one-time final act. Now justification or condemnation will take place in the eschatological day of
judgment, at which time the cosmic Lord will judge both his
people and all the world. The general legal context of the term
is easily seen in a passage in Romans. "Who shall bring any
charge against God's elect? It is God who justifies; who is to
condemn?" (Rom. 8:33–34).

This is the basic context for Paul's appropriation of the term.
Yet he so turns the pharisaic interpretation of justification on its
head that it would have been virtually unrecognizable. Certainly to the extent that it was recognizable it would have been
completely offensive to any serious pharisee, for several reasons.
First, the eschatological judgment is not in the future, but in its
deepest reality has already occurred—and not in some cosmic
display of power, but in the death of a legally executed criminal,
Jesus of Nazareth. We do not know exactly *how* Paul came to
identify this death with God's eschatological act, but the fact that
he does is clear enough (Rom. 3:21–26; 5:1, 9). Second, the
judgment is an act of universal justification—thus the judgment
is acquittal for all people. How unheard-of that God acquits
everybody! (Rom. 5:18). How could any sane person think of
the entire world as righteous? At least, universal righteousness
should be the only ground on which universal acquittal is con-
ceivable. But we already know that Paul believed all humanity
was in sin. Thus the opposite must be the case, that God has
universally acquitted sinful people. And this is, in fact, what
Paul says. Justification is justification of the impious (Rom.
4:5). The offensiveness of the scheme escalates! And that
means, finally, that justification is an act of sheer grace, of gift.
God has given persons life without any payment of moral deeds.

Let us reflect for a moment upon these momentous transformations. No one *has* to come before God's judgment seat with
achievements. No questions are asked about religious belief,

virtue, pious living, ethical heroics. Here there are places open for the worst monsters the human race has produced. But there is another side, more crucial and threatening to the majority of us. No one *can* come before God's judgment seat with belief or piety in hand. No one can boast in himself or herself, but only in God, for only God is the genuine source of authentic life. Everyone must stand naked before the God who graciously gives.

Here emerges the real threat. For if the tragic condition of humanity is anxiously to create structures and security of existence precisely in the act of achievement, Paul's proclamation is that salvation lies precisely in giving all of that project up. All that we grasped to ourselves must be willingly thrown away. No longer do we *have* to look over our shoulders to see what others think of us; we are liberated from that anxiety—but no longer *can* we use our place in the community to satisfy our self-assurance. Thrown away must be all the support gained from our carefully constructed life-facade—business skills, intellectual accomplishments, community esteem, and especially our ethical performance, the most insidious and demonic crutch of all.

I sometimes ask my students to close their eyes and to think about what is so centrally important to them, what they clutch to their hearts most of all, which if they had to give up they would be forced to consider suicide. It is a useful exercise, if done honestly, because it forces us to think at the depth of human existence in which Paul's thought is moving. There have been moments in my own life when it seemed almost certain that all I had striven for would suddenly be lost, that I would be stripped of everything that seemed important and everything that I had worked hard to achieve. Yet at those moments the assurance that my life was secure in God's hand sustained me with a liberating power that is indescribable. It is this dark night of the soul, this frightening abyss, where the grace of God can meet us and free us from the threat of meaninglessness and total loss. To know life as sheer gift is the greatest experience of freedom we can have.

And yet it seems to be that very act of grace which poses the threat! For if we cannot bring our treasured collection of achievement into the kingdom of God, then is not grace the threat of nonexistence, since I have so completely identified myself with the project which has created these achievements? To leave them outside the door is so to denude my being that I may not have anything left. Dare I take the chance? What is there to prove that Paul's gospel is right? Maybe I should hang on at least to a few things, just in case. But Paul is adamant. When he says God justifies *only* by grace, he means it all the way. No compromise is possible, because compromise in this instance is actually capitulation to sin, that is, to justification by works.

Thus Paul's theology of justification by grace is so radical as to be ultimately liberating, ultimately offensive, and ultimately threatening: liberating because we are free from the world; offensive because the moral standards so important to the world are torn down—is not this anarchy in the Godhead itself?; and threatening because it *seems* to threaten death, rather than to offer life. Most people clearly are not willing to take such a big risk; they prefer to continue to clutch at their achievements. But Paul, at least, is clear about the matter. To continue to clutch, even at moral virtue, is sin.

THE ESCHATOLOGICAL CREATION

What is emerging is a radical *either/or,* a description of the culture of sin and the culture of grace as two completely different worlds. And this would mean that to leave sin and enter grace is like leaving one world and entering another that is totally different. In fact, this is the way Paul himself describes it. In this he is, as in the motifs described earlier, dependent upon Jewish ideas; yet at the same time he radically transforms them.

We have seen that Jewish eschatology placed the time of Israel entering into eternal life in the future, eschatological day of judgment. In one sense, this was also seen as leaving one world and entering another, although there were certainly correspondences between this world and the next, eschatological, perfect world. Thus eternal life was, from the perspective of this life, a postponed reality.

But Paul, while he accepted the sharp division between this world and the world of eternal life, claimed that that new world had already broken into the present time and was in the church an already existing reality. This world—by which he means the culture of sin and death—is passing away (1 Cor. 7:31). "There-

fore, if any one is in Christ, he is a new creation; the old has
passed away, behold, the new has come" (2 Cor. 5:17). "For
neither circumcision counts for anything, nor uncircumcision,
but a new creation" (Gal. 6:15). The act of God in Christ has
done much more than merely acquit the sinner; it has created
the possibility of living in a new world, radically different from
the culture of sin and death. And this possibility is not reserved,
postponed, for the future; it is a *present* possibility, which Paul
sees actually realized in the church.

Thus justification is not to be equated with forgiveness for
sin. Paul uses the word *forgiveness* hardly at all, and the reason
is clear.[18] What Paul is describing is not simply an order, a
world, in which people fail, are forgiven, and then try harder.
Justification throws one into an entirely different order or world,
which lives out of a totally different reality. There is, in fact, a
kind of condemnation involved in the eschatological judgment as
Paul sees it. It is not a condemnation of persons, but a condemnation of the reality which these persons had accepted as,
somehow, ontologically true. God's act in Christ shows up that
world to be a false reality, constructed not by God but by persons
too anxious and timid to trust God.

The new, eschatological reality, brought into existence by
God's act in Christ, is totally different. Paul shows what is the
quality of this new world: "For Christ is the end [the finish] of
the law, that every one who has faith may be justified" (Rom.
10:4).[19] The culture of sin and death was founded on justification by works, or the "performance principle." The new world is
based on justification by faith, the *finis* (end) of the law as a
system of salvation. In this new world persons accept their life as
a gift from God, not as something to be earned. The system of
law is absent from the new world; that system has been destroyed
in the cross of Christ. And it is precisely this shift from justification by works to justification by grace that enables the shift from

18. Similarly Paul does not stress the motif of *sacrifice* when he is speaking
about the death of Jesus. That was a very early idea in the church, and
Paul shows he is acquainted with the idea. His own interpretation of the
death is, however, rooted in the motif of justification.

19. The Greek word Paul uses here, *telos*, can mean either *actual end*, or
consummation, goal. Some scholars argue that in Rom. 10:4 it has this
latter meaning. I do not think it un-Pauline to think of Jesus as the consummation of the promises in the Torah; but the context of the verse seems
to me strongly to indicate that here Paul means *finis*.

the culture of sin and death to that of the new creation to take place. Moreover, it is a shift whose reality can be experienced in this life, now.

This initial chapter has, of course, raised many questions not yet answered. They will be treated in the following chapters. Here I have only one final point to add, and it is the point which justifies the title of the chapter. When Paul speaks of a *new* creation, he is setting in tension two Jewish theological symbols —creation and *eschaton*. Again he shows himself dependent upon rabbinic theology, perhaps better stated here as mythology. The rabbis dwelled at length upon the first couple as persons created in the image of God and therefore potentially perfect. The rabbis enjoyed enlarging upon the story of Adam in Genesis, bestowing upon him all the traits of perfection they could imagine. After Adam sinned, these traits of perfection were taken away by God as punishment. When these same theologians began speculating about what persons would be like in the kingdom of God, what eschatological existence would be like, they described it in precisely the same terms they used to describe Adam's perfection before his sin and fall.[20] And that suggests something of the utmost importance. When they spoke about eschatological existence they were thinking of eternal life as being not something completely estranged from human nature, not some reality that was beyond humanity, not salvation *out of* humanity. They saw it rather as salvation back into humanity, as restoration to that reality which God had given the original Adam, and thus as salvation *into* authentic human existence.

Paul has picked up this idea from the rabbis and it determines his language about the new creation. God's intent in creation was not defective; he did not design humanity in one way, only to promise a different, higher superhumanity for eternal life. What God has always intended for persons is authentic human life. This authentic human life has been distorted because of human anxiety. Thus for both Paul and the rabbis salvation is not *out of* but *into* authentic human existence. Where Paul differs is in claiming that *now, already* in Christ, this authentic existence is possible.

At last an answer is possible to the very urgent question about

20. Cf. Scroggs, *Last Adam*, pp. 46–52, 54–74.

the threat of self-destruction which emerges at the challenge to give up the clutching after achievements, the apparent death which comes when the self gives up all it has understood to be the self. The self of the culture of sin and death turns out to be only a pseudo-self, which has masked the self originally created by God. The passage from one world to the next does not destroy the *authentic* self. Rather it destroys the pseudo-self created by the project of self-justification and thus allows the genuine self, that human person intended by God, actually to come into existence. Thus eschatological selfhood is the return, the restoration to original, authentic, human reality. The way ahead, into eternal life, thus turns out to be the way back, the restoration to creational humanity as designed by God.

Thus "salvation" for Paul turns out to be a distinctly human possibility, something which has always lain dormant within us, waiting to be brought into existence by God's act in Christ. It is, to return to the paradoxical title of this chapter, eschatological creation. In one sense it is *creatio ex nihilo*, as the passage I close with suggests. But it is the very same *creatio ex nihilo* which was God's creative and redeeming activity at the beginning.

> For consider your call, brethren; not many of you were wise according to worldly standards, not many were powerful, not many were of noble birth; but God chose what is foolish in the world to shame the wise, God chose what is weak in the world to shame the strong, God chose what is low and despised in the world, **even things that are not**, to bring to nothing things that are, so that no human being might boast in the presence of God. He is the source of your life in Christ Jesus, whom God made our wisdom, our righteousness and sanctification and redemption; therefore, as it is written, "Let him who boasts, boast of the Lord." [1 Cor. 1:26–31; emphasis mine]

2

Faith:
Eschatological Existence

Through Christ the new aeon has burst into the present. "If any
one is in Christ he is a new creation" (2 Cor. 5:17). And yet, as
we saw, the label of this eschatological reality as new *creation*
points the way back to God's intent in the original creation, an
intent which, because he created a humanity free to sin, was
thwarted by human anxiety and obstinacy. But what does all
that language mean, really? If it *does* mean something, there
ought to be something different about human existence. The
possibility of human participation in eschatological existence
must be a real and indeed realizable possibility. And so we must
turn to ask Paul what he means by the new creation bursting
into the present. In short, what does he think eschatological
existence looks like?

This is not, of course, to shortchange what Paul says about the
future. There is to be, he is convinced, a heavenly kingdom of
God in which the redeemed will forever participate in their spiritual bodies. Paul here is simply sharing typical apocalyptic
beliefs, and there is nothing particularly startling, given his time
and place, about these affirmations. What *is* startling is the
unheard-of claim that the kingdom is anything more than future,
a claim which I believe goes back to Jesus himself, and a claim
which Paul shared with many other early Christians. The question before us is, *What forced Paul and his fellow believers to
affirm any sort of present eschatology?* The answer must be that
there was something so distinctive about their new life as believ-

ers that they knew no other way to talk about it except in eschatological terms. Language can, of course, be traditional, and thus abstract, and perhaps even meaningless. Traditional language may have nothing to do with human experiences. When the traditional language system is broken, however, as traditional Jewish apocalyptic language was broken by the early Christians, it must reflect something in experience which causes the break. Otherwise the change in language is inexplicable. Thus it is in Paul's language about present eschatology that we are to seek his understanding of basic Christian reality.

The language about future consummation does, however, have an important function in Pauline theology. Paul knows that there is a *not yet* as well as a *now*. The *not yet* comes into play against believers who pridefully boast that they are already consummated; it guards against the temptation to think that one already possesses complete salvation so that *whatever* one is or does is eschatological. The possibility of falling out of the new creation back into the old is a constant threat, and Paul would not have his congregations forget it. Eschatological existence *is* an actualized reality for Paul; but his *not yet* maintains that realistic perspective which acknowledges that we are all falling into doubt and anxiety over and over again and have constantly to return to the source of life, constantly to be restored to life in grace.

Our task is, then, to attempt to discover how Paul describes present eschatological existence, what the various dimensions of its reality are. But first I would like to claim the assistance of Norman O. Brown's interpretation of Freud, for this may help us be more sensitive to what Paul is saying. In Freud's analysis of the human condition, the result of the child's march through the stages of sexual organization, from the original undifferentiated narcissism through oral, anal, and phallic periods, is, as far as Brown is concerned, essentially tragic. The libido is repressed, although it can never be destroyed; the superego tyrannically rules over the self and stores up aggression turned inward. The reality principle has replaced the pleasure principle, and this means that any hope for gratification is postponed indefinitely into the future. Only the conscious ego has a possibility of real life; but for Freud this part of the self is the weakest of all; "a poor creature," he calls it.[1] Furthermore, Freud believed the ego *should* be instructed by the reality principle and accept the necessity of renunciation. Humanity would never, in his views, ever be a happy humanity. Indeed, with the constant push of the death drives, the continued existence of civilization itself is questionable. The best hope is the compromise of mature renunciation, the ego cooperating with the reality principle and, where necessary, psychiatry. After Freud has built up his theory of the death and love drives, this pessimism is grounded ontologically, since the process of sexual organization and the constant pressure of aggression are now based in the very nature of living organisms.[2]

Brown's reinterpretation of Freud is something of an intellectual tour de force; yet I believe that it is justified and that it throws open exciting new possibilities of understanding. Contrary to many post-Freudians, Brown accepts Freud's later theories about the death and love drives, although he acknowledges some inconsistencies in Freud's argument. But there is, Brown argues, a basic flaw in the conclusions Freud has drawn. The movement through the stages of sexual organization is based, Brown argues, on fantasy, not reality.[3] The infant is not going to die when separated momentarily from the mother; the father does not really wish to kill the child. There is no *ontological* reason why the libido has to be repressed, or why the superego has aggressively to restrict the affections and desire of the child. Surely there is the death drive; but Brown attributes the movement through sexual organization to be based not on the pressure of the death drive, but rather on fear of death; the movement is a *flight from death*, either back to the womb or forward toward genital sexuality.

Brown's friends and enemies thus come out to be mostly different from Freud's. Brown's enemies are all the repressive mechanisms, the superego (which also became an enemy in Freud), and the reality principle. Brown wants to celebrate the possibil-

1. Sigmund Freud, *The Ego and the Id*, ed. James Strachey and trans. Joan Riviere (New York: W. W. Norton, 1974), p. 46.
2. Sigmund Freud, *Beyond the Pleasure Principle*, trans. James Strachey (New York: Liveright, 1970) and *Civilization and Its Discontents* (New York: W. W. Norton, 1961).
3. Norman O. Brown, *Life Against Death* (Middletown, Ct.: Wesleyan University Press, 1959), pp. 110–34.

ity of gratification and thinks he has found a way where this is in a mature and legitimate way possible. If the result of the child's development is based on fantasy, then it should be possible to conceive of a way of overcoming that result, since there is now no ontological necessity for that condition. And for Brown the way out is a way back: a movement back behind the stages of sexual organization to unrepressed libido, to a narcissism which is not self-seeking but joyous union with the world. It is an erotic mode of being, but *eros* is not to be equated with *sexuality* in any sense in which we are accustomed to think of that term. The process of sexual organization has, in fact, restricted the force of the libido to genital sexuality and to limited objects. Thus in a very real sense the flight from death is the cause of sex in our normal use of the term *sex*. The erotic mode of being (erotic exuberance, Brown calls it), that which lies behind the process of sexual organization, diffuses the libido back to its original scope, so that the self opens itself to the inclusive community of the world.[4]

Thus it is not a selfish mode of being. Brown distinguishes erotic exuberance both from the Platonic notion of eros and the Christian notion of agape. "The Platonic Eros is the child of defect or want. Its direction is away from the insufficient self; its aim is to possess the object which completes it." Agape, on the other hand, while basing itself in the insufficiency of the self, aims at extinguishing the self. "From the psychoanalytical point of view, Platonic Eros is inseparable from an aggressive component, Christian Agape inseparable from a masochistic component." By contrast, "the self-activity and self-enjoyment of the narcissistic Eros must consist in an overflow outward into the world" (p. 49). It is the desire for union without possession.

Brown's thought is at times tortuously complex and I cannot here pursue it further. But I hope I have said enough to suggest that from a psychoanalytic perspective it is possible to have at least a vision of a humanity which realizes in joy and love a full and authentic existence. The vision points the way back behind the distortions of history to restore people to true selfhood. It is a genuinely eschatological vision, and it is hardly accidental that Brown titles his last chapter "The Resurrection of the Body."

4. Ibid., pp. 49, 110–34.

Here the author describes what his eschatological humanity would look like. It is a return to wholeness, the putting back together of body and soul, an end to the repression of both life and death, for realization of this return is made possible only by the acceptance of death. It is a life which returns to its original fullness and does not have to strive to earn salvation (for Brown and Paul equally, an impossible project). Performance principle and postponement principle are not a part of Brown's kingdom of God.[5]

Again I have to confess that for me these correlations between Brown and Paul are striking and, when I first realized them, startling. I am convinced that both are pointing to the same vision of authentic human reality. The language systems are totally different, but that should not deter us from using the insights of one to understand the other. Where Paul departs from Brown is over the means by which this restoration can take place. Brown seemingly has no options apart from human thinking and willing; for Paul, of course, only through God in Christ can the transformation take place. But the striking thing to observe here is that the direction and the process are similar. For both Brown and Paul, authentic life consists in a return to an original situation made possible by the risk taken of giving up striving for selfhood and by accepting selfhood, rather, as something already present. The quality of this new but original life is one of self-acceptance, love, and joy.

FAITH

When Paul says the believer in Christ is in a new creation, and when he says that the old world, the old creation, is passing away, he is, we have seen, speaking of the act of salvation as enabling the person to leave one world and enter another. While there is continuity between God's intent in creation and his realization of this intent in the eschatological community, Paul sees a radical *discontinuity* between the ordinary world of history in which mankind is rooted and that new world now brought into existence.

---

5. In a profound way, Norman O. Brown has moved beyond his vision of the resurrected body in *Love's Body* (New York: Random House, 1966). But there is no opportunity here to discuss this movement.

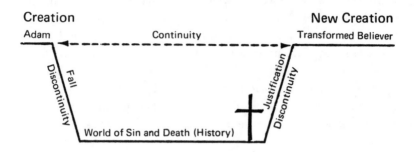

The reality of the culture of sin and death, based on anxiety, performance principle, justification by works or knowledge, or whatever, is a totally different reality from that world which lives out of justification by grace. Everything becomes new. One group of theologians calls this world-switching a "radical perceptual shift."[6] By this they mean that the very roots of a person's thinking, the way the world is looked at, perceived, and thus lived in, is turned upside down.

The term which Paul uses to describe this living in the new world is *faith*. Faith is not for Paul primarily a series of intellectual, theological propositions, as the term has come to mean in our tradition. Faith is rather that basic stance before the God of grace; it is a quality of existence, indeed that quality of existence in the new creation. It is the constant confidence that God has given us our life as sheer gift. It is the courage to remain standing in that place, not to be scared by anxiety, fear, or lack of trust into returning to that old creation based on justification by works. Faith is thus the basic attitude of the believer toward God. And only this stance produces eschatological existence. Paul says it clearly: "Whatever does not come from faith is sin" (Rom. 14:23).

Thus the basic theological program of Paul is summed up in

6. S. Daniel Batson, C. Beker, and M. Clark, *Commitment without Ideology* (Philadelphia: United Church Press, 1973). These authors confess dependence upon Peter Berger and Thomas Luckmann, *The Social Construction of Reality* (Garden City, N.Y.: Doubleday, 1966). I have also found the tools of the sociology of knowledge used by Berger and Luckmann tremendously helpful in my analysis.

these three terms, *justification* by *grace* through *faith*. Justification by grace is God's creative act of salvation; faith is that
quality of existence of the saved person. Thus we must be careful not to misunderstand Paul when he sometimes drops the
second term, *grace*, and speaks of justification by or through
faith, as if some future salvation comes through accepting a series
of beliefs now—as if it meant "faith now, salvation later." The
eschatological mode of being is faith, and faith *is* salvation.

Salvation is sheer gift and is a gift for all. But how then can
we explain the tension in Paul's thought between the universal-
ity of the gift of God and his awareness that not everybody comes
to faith? (Contrast Rom. 5:18 and 1 Cor. 15:22 with 2 Cor.
4:3–4.) The solution is that the gift has to be accepted before it
has any effect. Just as I get no benefit from a gift unless I untie
the wrapping, open the box, and use the gift, so providing me
with the *possibility* of a new mode of existence still demands my
accepting that possibility and living out of it.

In order better to understand the nuances of faith, we might
explore two related facets. It is often said that faith is closely
related to obedience, that it has the characteristic of faithfulness.
This is true, but then we have to see how Paul defines obedience. Speaking of the Jews who refused to become believers in
Christ, he writes, "For being ignorant of the justification which
comes from God, and seeking to stand in their own, they did not
become obedient to that justification from God" (Rom. 10:3).
Here *disobedience is the refusal to accept justification by grace
through faith*; it is continuing to live as if the gift of life were
something to be worked for. Thus disobedience applies to the
righteous pharisee as he strives for perfect fulfillment of the
Torah. Yes, faith *is* practically synonymous with obedience, but
obedience does not mean dogged attention to, and following of, a
certain set of commandments, but rather is defined as willingness
to live before that gracious God who bestows life freely as sheer
gift. To remain in that posture *is* obedience.

It is also suggested often that faith has a relation to trust.
Again this is true, but again we have to listen carefully to Paul's
understanding. In Romans 4 he wishes to give an example of a
person of faith. Amazingly enough, he does not exhibit a Chris-

tian, not even some pillar of the church like Peter; he points instead toward Abraham as, in Kierkegaard's term, "the knight of faith." He picks up the story in Genesis of God's promise to Abraham that he would be the father of a great nation. But Abraham is childless. He is, moreover, too old to father a child. His wife, Sarah, is not only that; she has always been barren. How could Abraham realistically trust God's promise? But according to Paul's reading of the story, he did; Abraham "grew strong in his faith as he gave glory to God, fully convinced that God was able to do what he had promised" (Rom. 4:20-21). Paul then applies that trust to contemporary believers, those who have faith in the God who raised Jesus Christ. The trust is thus in something that is real, but about which there can be no proof, and furthermore about something that flies in the face of what one normally expects. Trust is confidence in that reality despite the fact that the world suggests that confidence to be unwarranted.

Abraham trusted that he would have a child, despite the fact that from what he knew of the world it would be impossible. Christians have confidence that the liberating act of God's justification by grace is real despite the fact that it came in the death of a common, legally executed criminal. In the world, things don't happen this way. Applied to the analysis we are making, faith is trust in the sense that the faithful person confidently lives his or her life as gift, despite the fact that such a mode of being is totally foreign to the way people in the old world live their lives. The culture of sin and death is confident that its ways are right. Conversely, it is convinced that basing life on God's sheer gift is dangerous, foolish, and ultimately self-destructive. Paul's believer, nevertheless, trusts that living life as gift is indeed according to God's creational intent.

Since, however, this faith is an experienced, concrete reality, a felt and perceived existence of which the individual is aware, this trust is in no way a dogged, rigid determination to remain in that posture at all costs. Such a rigidity would only indicate that the present reality has disappeared and everything is again postponed. In faith that is *present* existence there is something joyously self-authenticating about that reality.

CHARACTERISTICS OF ESCHATOLOGICAL EXISTENCE

So far, then, we have tried to understand what Paul means when he speaks about faith as eschatological existence. Now I would like to hold up for attention some specific characteristics of this faithful life, to see if we can learn more about what such a life would be like. Perhaps it would be more accurate to say these characteristics are the *results* of faith.

Freedom. Freedom is a key word in the Pauline vocabulary and a crucial component of his theology of justification by grace. He exhorts the Galatians, "For freedom Christ has set us free; stand fast therefore and do not submit again to a yoke of slavery" (Gal. 5:1). And to the Corinthians: "Now the Lord is the Spirit, and where the Spirit of the Lord is, there is freedom" (2 Cor. 3:17).

What are we freed from? All sorts of things: freed from the old world and that part of it which is our own past history; freed from what people think about us; freed from what we think about ourselves, either positively or negatively. Thus we are freed from the agony of failure and the tense striving for success, either in memory or in prospect. We are freed from the tyranny of someone else's claim about what is true and what is morally correct behavior. We are freed from the claim that some set of rules and regulations is ontologically true and eternally binding. We are even freed from the fear of going to hell unless we can subscribe to a given set of theological dogmas. As Paul says, it is more important to be known (by God) than to know.

In the correspondence with the Corinthians he discusses with them a problem they were worrying about, namely, whether a Christian could eat meat sold in the marketplace (which had, presumably, been a part of pagan sacrifices according to the usual Greek custom). Some believers felt it was immoral to buy and eat such meat. Paul has no such problem. "Eat whatever is sold in the meat market without raising any question on the ground of conscience. 'For the earth is the Lord's, and everything in it' " (1 Cor. 10:25–26). Now those of you who know the context know that this is not the end of the matter (to this we will return in chapter 4), but his basic judgment is quite clear. The Christian is freed from this kind of pietistic scruple, or as one might say, anxiety. In Romans, in response to the question of which, if any, days should be considered holy by the Christian, his answer is that one is free to choose for himself or herself. "Let every one be fully convinced in his own mind" (Rom. 14:5). Paul is himself so flexible in his observance of rules and regulations that he can be as a Greek to Greeks and a Jew to Jews (1 Cor. 9:19–23).

And whence comes this freedom? Squarely out of the constant confidence which is faith in the God who gives life. "It is God who justifies; who is to condemn?" (Rom. 8:33–34). As long as I hold securely to the knowledge that God has given me my life, no thing or person or community or state can take that confidence away from me and make me anxiously bow to its own standards. This is the ultimate root of that incredible freedom to die for one's faith. It is also the root of the freedom to be for others. This leads us to the awareness that the most important freedom, ultimately, is freedom *for others*, but discussion of this must wait until chapter 4.

Joy. It may surprise you to learn that the various words for joy and rejoicing assemble to make a very large word group in Paul's vocabulary. For a person who was so buffeted about by the outside world, it is remarkable that the Apostle was so aware of this reality. When writing the letter to the Philippians, at which point he knew he might be shortly executed, he writes, "Rejoice in the Lord always; again I will say, Rejoice" (Phil. 4:4). This rejoicing can be theological ("Rejoice in your hope" [Rom. 12:12]). But it can also be unabashedly personal. Paul enjoyed his friends, missed them when he was separated from them, and rejoiced when they returned. "I rejoice at the coming of Stephanas and Fortunatus and Achaicus, because they have made up for your absence; for they refreshed my spirit as well as yours" (1 Cor. 16:17–18). In writing to the Thessalonians Paul reveals the anxiety that he felt at one time when he was away from them and had heard no word. He sends Timothy all the way from Athens to get a report, and when Timothy returns with welcome news, Paul almost explodes in rhetorical fullness. "For what thanksgiving can we render to God for you, for all the joy which

we feel for your sake before our God . . . ?" (1 Thess. 3:9).
Somewhat the same thing happened in another situation involving the Corinthian church. Titus arrives with welcome news
which has resolved a tense situation in Paul's favor. "But God,
who comforts the downcast, comforted us by the coming of Titus,
and not only by his coming but also by the comfort with which he
was comforted in you, as he told us of your longing, your mourning, your zeal for me, so that I rejoiced still more" (2 Cor. 7:6–7).
Eschatological existence, far from being the morose life of the
anxious pietist, is full of robust joy.

Peace. Another important and often-repeated word for Paul is
peace. This, of course, goes back to his Jewish heritage. As such
it appears prominently in his salutation and benedictions. But
in the Christian Paul the word is filled with unusual intensity.
"And the peace of God, which passes all understanding, will
keep your hearts and your minds in Christ Jesus" (Phil. 4:7).
"Therefore, since we are justified by faith, we have peace with
God through our Lord Jesus Christ" (Rom. 5:1). Here it is clear
that peace is the fruit of justification. To accept the Spirit results in peace (Rom. 8:6). In instructing the Corinthians to
accept a divorce in a mixed marriage if the unbelieving partner
wishes the separation, he gives as his warrant, "For God has
called us to peace" (1 Cor. 7:15). In dealing with worship services which are getting out of hand, he counsels, "For God is not
a God of confusion but of peace" (1 Cor. 14:33).

In Judaism this word has a serious theological connotation. It
denotes the serenity which stems from Israel's right relationship
with God. Paul knows this serenity, a serenity felt by persons
being not only at peace with God but with themselves as well.
Peace is almost a synonym of *reconciliation*; the hostility between
persons and God is over now in Christ; as a result of reconciliation people can be at peace with the God of peace. It is the
profound sense, reaching to the roots of Christian existence, that
nothing "will be able to separate us from the love of God in
Christ Jesus our Lord" (Rom. 8:39).

Love. I have reserved until now discussion about love, because I wanted to make it clear that it is by no means the only
key word Paul uses to describe eschatological existence. Chris-

tian existence is not exhausted in one word or one concept. Nevertheless, love is the single most important word. The question, however, is what Paul means when he uses the term *agape*. The issue is complex because in recent years we have been bombarded with a presumed contrast between eros and agape, with extravagant claims that Christian love is somehow unique and superior to other forms of loving.[7] These claims, in my judgment, are based on bad psychology, bad theology, and bad exegesis. It is, to be sure, unfair to make such sweeping negative judgments without a detailed analysis which is impossible here. I must restrict myself to two generalizing affirmations.

First, if understood in the way Brown defines *eros*, there is nothing improper, exegetically or theologically, in calling Christian love "erotic." The heavy use of the word-family *agape* in the New Testament in preference to other possible words has *no* theological meaning; it is simply a reflex of the semantic background of the writers.[8] Paul, as we have already suggested, is filled with yearning in his affection for fellow workers and churches. Far from reflecting base elements in human nature, desire signals a positive evaluation of the other person, as long as it is not rooted in the neurotic and demonic need to use and dominate other people. That means that healthy yearning and appreciation of others is based in justification by grace.

It is extremely interesting to see Paul's exegesis of the famous verse in Leviticus, "You shall love your neighbor as yourself" (Lev. 19:18). The two times he cites it, he says it means "loving one another" (Rom. 13:8; Gal. 5:13–14). That is, it is taken to refer to *mutuality* within the community of love. To love and *be loved* are thus legitimized at the same moment. Let me remind you of Brown's judgment that the Christian notion of agape is filled with masochistic components. If agape is defined as so-called disinterested love, the charge is, I think, true. But it is not true for Paul's idea of love, which fits Brown's description of love as joyous union with the world, in which the self is not annihilated but fulfilled.

7. The most famous proponent of such a view is Anders Nygren, *Agape and Eros* (Philadelphia: Westminster, 1953).
8. *Agape* was already the primary word for love in the Greek translation of the Old Testament, and was used for every phenomenon from rape to God's love for Israel.

The second affirmation is that Paul's awareness of the non-aggressive character of love needs to be emphasized. This may seem to be surprising; by definition love cannot be aggressive! And yet how much aggression is customarily concealed under the facade of "love." "I love you, I know what is best for you, so do what I say," is more frequent in much so-called loving than we might care to admit. And that is pure aggression. How often does love say, "I told you so," with its covert glee at the misfortune of the "love." How much explicit sex, including that within the marriage bed, is an expression of aggression! "To love" so often means "to dominate." I would almost be so bold as to say that in that reality of human existence based upon justification by works, upon the need to work to secure the self, love is *primarily* an aggressive act, since all people, including the closest to us, are vehicles for our project of self-salvation.

With this as a background, I hardly need to argue that Paul is different. I only have to quote a few verses from his famous hymn to love: "Love is patient and kind; love is not jealous or boastful; it is not arrogant or rude. Love does not insist on its own way; it is not irritable or resentful; it does not rejoice at wrong, but rejoices in the right. Love bears all things, believes all things, hopes all things, endures all things" (1 Cor. 13:4–7).

With an incredible insight Paul contrasts true love with all those aggressive realities that make up life in this world. Persons, freed by grace, can love without that anxiety which inevitably ends in aggression.

Eschatological existence and the human body. One problem we cannot avoid is the role of the physical body in present eschatological existence. The contrast between current interest in reclaiming the integrated self—body, emotions, mind—and the popular sense that Paul is just at this point particularly repressive means that the issue must be confronted head on. We must keep clear, however, just which model of the integrated self we wish to accept. On the one hand, there is that which we might call the "*Playboy* image," with its aggressive and genitally (but also orally and anally) oriented sexuality. Paul would, of course, have little in common with that model. But Paul's aversion to such a model would be equally shared by Norman O. Brown, who presents us with a totally different model of integration, the diffused and ethically oriented erotic exuberance which seeks union with the world without any attempt at domination. With *this* model there is commonality in Paul.

Paul, it must first be admitted, does not envision corporeality in the world of the final consummation. The resurrected body will be a "spiritual" body. Now it is possible to correlate Paul's meaning of *spiritual* with a diffused eros. The Spirit is the source of one's total being and act in Christ; thus it is one way of speaking about the source of love in a nonsexual manifestation. Nevertheless, the spiritual body is certainly for Paul a noncorporeal body.

The question which concerns us, however, is the role of the body in the present situation where the believer remains in the corporeal state and yet is also graced with the Spirit and already exists in the new creation. Are a person's emotional and bodily expressions irrelevant to Christian existence, as some of the Corinthians perhaps believed? Or is the other extreme the correct one—that believers should repress their emotions and body as somehow inferior to their spiritual existence, as some others among the Corinthians seem to have thought?

As so often happens, Paul refuses to take either extreme, and his dialectic pushes him to a complex but more acceptable position. One thing is clear. The early church did not sit on, or repress, emotions. The emotional pitch of the church, in fact, was intense. This was perhaps especially true of the Pauline churches. Glossolalia, or speaking in tongues, was one example of this intensity. Of course this could be overdone, and Paul tells the Corinthians in effect to "cool it," but he can at the same time say to them, "I thank God that I speak in tongues more than you all" (1 Cor. 14:18). Without making judgments on the theological reality of glossolalia, the phenomenon can at least be understood as the intense release of repressed emotion, in a context in which the person trusts the situation so that the release can take place and have a positive function. Outside of the community it may still be necessary to repress one's feelings, but in the context of the eschatological community such release has its place.

A contemporary example may help us understand this dynamic. In a poignant chapter in his book *Migrants, Mountaineers and Sharecroppers* Robert Coles describes the interior life of the religious dimension of these dispossessed and alienated Americans.[9] For these folk, religion is about the one positive dimension in an otherwise well-nigh intolerable world. In the many heartrending quotes drawn from the agony of these people, Coles communicates the centrality of the church meeting and the free emotional expression which frequently occurs. Speaking in tongues is a common feature in these services. But even when it isn't, the service acts as a catalyst to release the feelings of these people and to reintegrate them, to restore emotions to mind and body.

Just a few examples:

> I wait all week for Sunday. That's the day that counts, you know. It's the only day of the week for me, the one day when **we** count, because then God is there, beckoning you, telling you it's all right, just come on over and be with Me, be with Me for a few minutes. [pp. 580–81]

> He'll [the minister] get us singing and get us talking and get us confessing, and pretty soon you won't know if you've been there a day or a week. All you know is that you're paying attention, because it's the most important thing in your life to do so, and it's what counts. [p. 591]

> I come out of there and I'm taller. I'm feeling bigger. I feel God has taken me to Him. He put His hand on my shoulder, and said, "Brother John Wilson, the reason that I want you praying to me is so you won't be looking at yourself and feeling so low. Brother John, it stands to reason that if I'm going to be looking after you, then you're OK, yes you are, and don't let anyone tell you otherwise." [pp. 596–97]

Similar feelings must have been common within the Pauline churches. In the situation at Corinth the worship meetings seem to have gotten out of hand, and Paul laments the disorder. He never, however, denies the validity of the emotional expression itself. The very letters themselves are rich in emotional expression; Paul is as free to express his anger as his love. His em-

9. Robert Coles, *Children of Crisis: Migrants, Mountaineers and Sharecroppers* (Boston: Little, Brown & Co., 1971).

pathetic urges are captured in the phrase, "Who is weak, and I am
not weak? Who is made to fall, and I am not indignant?" (2
Cor. 11:29). He encourages others to do the same: "Rejoice with
those who rejoice, weep with those who weep" (Rom. 12:15).
The apparently contrary statement in 1 Corinthians 7:30 is to be
taken as an injunction not to allow worldly things to assume the
ultimate place, rather than as repression of emotion: "Let . . .
those who mourn [live] as though they were not mourning, and
those who rejoice as though they were not rejoicing."

Paul never gives the corporeal body pride of place or even
much of a right, independent of the self as a larger whole
("'Food is meant for the stomach and the stomach for food'—
and God will destroy both one and the other" [1 Cor. 6:13]).
Nevertheless, when the body *is* an expression of the larger self,
then Paul does take it seriously and adopts neither a gnostic
indifference nor a pietistic asceticism. Paul's view is here consonant with the "diffused eros" of the psychoanalytic vision.
The body-self is to be an expression of love for the total community.

In 1 Corinthians 7 Paul is dealing with some questions about
marriage and divorce put to him by the church. Paul is himself
not married and considers this the best situation for the believer.
Yet he in no way condemns marriage, and within marriage
considers the sexual relation not simply possible but, indeed,
indispensable. In fact he explicitly directs the married couple
toward sexual relationships.[10] If this is so, then why does he
think an unmarried state best for the believer?

In verses 32–35 he gives what I take to be the answer. "The
unmarried man is anxious about the affairs of the Lord, how to
please the Lord; but the married man is anxious about worldly
affairs, how to please his wife, and his interests are divided" (1
Cor. 7:32–34). The question here is, What are "the affairs of
the Lord"? From the context these affairs must refer to the
believing community; the service due to the Lord is a whole-
hearted, total attention directed toward the church. Paul here
votes the *in*clusive community (the church) to be of greater importance than the *ex*clusive (the marriage). Here is Paul's
"diffused eros," the self, unshackled from genital organization,

10. Cf. the discussion below, pp. 72–73.

now freed to direct its energies toward the larger community, the church. Yet within this diffused eros, genital sexuality does have its place in the community of marriage. Outside of marriage, genital sexuality is forbidden. To commit adultery or to go to a prostitute defiles the person. Even this shows that bodily expressions are part of Christian existence. Mind, soul, and body are a unity and through them all the self can express eschatological existence.

CONCLUSION

There are other dimensions of eschatological existence we could discuss, but I want to end with a magnificent generalizing list provided by Paul himself. In Galatians 5 Paul contrasts life in this world with eschatological existence. The first he captions as works of the flesh (by which he means activity of the total self, not just corporeal activities); the latter, as fruit of the spirit. "But the fruit of the Spirit is love, joy, peace, patience, kindness, goodness, faithfulness, gentleness, self-control"[11] (Gal. 5:22–23). What a list of unaggressive, loving, caring values. And do I need point out that in any sexist handbook these would be labeled "feminine virtues"? For Paul they are descriptions of all human eschatological persons!

None of this is to deny Paul's poignant awareness of the imperfection of believers and the often brutally expressed hostility of the world of sin and death. In fact it is difficult to conceive of a ministry more acquainted with sorrows than Paul's own. Imprisonment, physical torture, hunger, exposure, and shipwreck are among Paul's encounters with the savagery of the world (2 Cor. 11:23–33). Presumably these ultimately cost him his very life. When confronted by the boasting of his opponents, the apostle in an intense outburst of irony even claims to boast only about his misfortunes, his weakness (2 Cor. 11:30; 12:5). His outburst, however, should not be read as self-hatred, and knowledge of Paul's difficulties only makes his emphasis upon the

---

11. Self-control is, of course, a potentially repressive term; and Paul is certainly himself a disciplined person, using the analogy of a boxer in training on one occasion (1 Cor. 9:26–27). In itself, however, discipline is not contrary to the unrepressed life. It is hard to imagine a truly caring person without a commitment to discipline and self-control.

present possibility of Christian existence the more remarkable and important. Paul is no masochist who embraces suffering. When it is necessary he will accept it, but what he strives to bring into existence is the joyful and liberating life of faith.

I have tried in this chapter to bring together the various ways by which Paul describes that new life made possible by God's act in Christ and brought into reality in the believer who is willing to accept that life as sheer gift. Paul is forced, of course, to make this description with words that were common to the old world. But we must hear him as attempting to describe with these words a human reality totally different from that reality the world considers as real, important, valuable, and possible. It is a vision every bit as radical as that of Brown, and the more promising in that it claims not only a vision but a real and recognizable reality. But if Brown and Paul, from such different perspectives and from such different times, have seen the same vision, we may suppose that others have as well. I close with a visionary passage by T. S. Eliot, in which, as I hear him, he also points to that eschatological reality which is the subject of our discourse.

At the still point of the turning world, Neither flesh nor fleshless;
Neither from nor towards; at the still point, there the dance is,
But neither arrest nor movement. And do not call it fixity,
Where past and future are gathered. Neither movement from nor
        towards,
Neither ascent nor decline. Except for the point, the still point,
There would be no dance, and there is only the dance.
I can only say, *there* we have been: But I cannot say where.
And I cannot say, how long, for that is to place it in time.
The inner freedom from the practical desire,
The release from action and suffering, release from the inner
And the outer compulsion, yet surrounded
By a grace of sense, a white light still and moving,
Erhebung without motion, concentration
Without elimination, both a new world
And the old made explicit, understood
In the completion of its partial ecstasy,
The resolution of its partial horror.
                              "Burnt Norton" II, *The Four Quartets*

3

The Church:
Eschatological Community

According to Jewish theology, God is in relation primarily with a people, a community of faith. The individual believer is never seen as isolated from that community. Indeed, the individual is not complete as an isolated unit. For Paul, reflecting that background, the same can be equally said. The community is an indispensable reality and is the primary object of his missionary work.

Nor is this community a collection of isolated individuals. The whole is more than the sum of its parts. His metaphor of the church as a body consisting of different parts with different functions, but all equally necessary for the full activity of the body, makes this clear enough. Actually it works both ways. The individual is not complete apart from the community; the community suffers loss if an individual leaves or does not participate.

This is, I believe, theologically and existentially profound. If Christian authenticity exists in the *mutuality* of loving, then the community is absolutely essential if this authenticity is to come into being. The individual needs the caring and sustaining power of others, and it is not a sign of weakness for this to be admitted. The evidence suggests that even Paul felt, indeed celebrated, this need. The need is legitimate because God has created persons *for* community, and only within this sustaining community is his creation of authentic humanity complete. I do not mean to equate participation in community with something as superficial or rigid as weekly attendance at the local church. The community may be of a varied sort, and it can be communicated by means other than actual physical presence. Sometimes the community comes into being through reading the Bible or a sermon. At times we are forced to rely upon our memory to call the community into existence. There are times when nothing works and we are alone with God. Yet I think we sense then that something is missing, even if at that moment *necessarily* missing from our human personhood.

Furthermore, only the community of faith can fulfill our existence as participants in the new creation, because only there can we be sure of encountering that caring and sustaining new creation. It is that love which flows out from the eschatological community which completes our selfhood. Certainly we also must live among individuals who, and in communities which, belong to the old creation; and we probably spend a good bit of our life in such situations. I am certainly not advocating (nor would Paul) a monastic withdrawal. Nevertheless, if we really do experience that fullness which comes from the eschatological community, then we should experience life in the church as different from our participation in the culture of sin and death.

Recent findings in the sociology of knowledge may deepen our insight into the relation of the individual to the community. Here I largely depend upon the book *The Social Construction of Reality* by Peter Berger and Thomas Luckmann.[1] The infant is "given his world" by his parents, at first through nonverbal communication. But as soon as the child learns to understand language, language itself becomes the most important means of being taught a world. By being "given a world" I mean that the child grows up *assuming* that what its parents or significant others say is true, is indeed true. What the culture communicated by these others takes to be ontologically real is taken as such by the child. All of one's reality is so communicated and so assumed. This basic orientation to a world the authors call the process of *primary socialization*. This learning usually stays with the individual throughout his or her life. He or she rarely

1. See Peter Berger and Thomas Luckmann, *The Social Construction of Reality* (Garden City, N.Y.: Doubleday, 1966), esp. pp. 129–63.

doubts it. The opposite to the Cartesian project thus occurs. Descartes bracketed all assumptions of truth and doubted everything. Ordinarily, however, we assume the truth of our world and bracket doubt (pp. 129–37).

The person continues to learn in school, in the army, in clubs. This kind of learning is called the process of *secondary socialization*. This learning can, of course, be called into question and replaced, and is not the same sort of learning as that of primary socialization. In a history class I learn that some of my former prejudices were unfounded, and so I discard them. Later on in a visit to Europe I may learn things that suggest the teacher in my class was not correct, and so I replace what I thought to be true by a new understanding (pp. 138–47).

But what can call into question my primary world, that world given me in my culture at large through the process of primary socialization? Something significant has to happen to cause me to doubt those basic presuppositions upon which that world is based—some crisis, perhaps some serious disfunction of the world I have assumed to be true. This may lead me to the conclusion that this world is not true after all, that some other truth appears more real. I may thus transform that basic world in which I have been living into a different world. Here is the radical perceptual shift we mentioned in the previous chapter. We have left the old world and entered a new one (pp. 156–57).

This transformation, or conversion, requires a process of *resocialization*. The first process of primary socialization has to be redone; the old world has to be destroyed and the new learned and internalized. And this process must be done in a social setting, that is, in a community. This new community must provide a "plausibility structure" which gives the new member confidence that his or her new world is in fact the truly real one (p. 157). This new community is the substitution for those significant others who mediated the old world to the infant. Speaking specifically of Paul's conversion, Berger and Luckmann write:

> To have a conversion experience is nothing much. The real thing is to be able to keep on taking it seriously; to retain a sense of its plausibility. **This** is where the religious community comes in. It

provides the indispensable plausibility structure for the new reality. In other words, Saul may have become Paul in the aloneness of religious ecstasy, but he could **remain** Paul only in the context of the Christian community that recognized him as such and confirmed the "new being" in which he now located this identity. [p. 158]

The need to confirm the new identity may lead the new community to cut off as much communication as possible with the old world and will certainly lead the new members to reinterpret his or her past from the perspective of the present (pp. 158–59). Thus it is that Paul understands Judaism radically differently *after* his conversion than he did before. In fact one can see the Epistle to the Romans as a gigantic reinterpretation of his religious past.[2] The pharisaic Saul could never have seen the history of Israel in such a manner.

One thing must be added. What the new community must communicate is not simply a *picture* of the new reality through language; what is even more important is to communicate that reality which the language expresses, namely that gift of God in Christ, which is justification by grace, and the power of love which can free the believer continually to live in faith in the God who gives life. All the *talk* about justification by grace can be impotent, if the *power* of love is missing.

CHARACTERISTICS OF THE
ESCHATOLOGICAL COMMUNITY

Just as in the previous chapter we attempted to describe some of the characteristics of the new individual's existence in Christ, so here we must raise the same question about the community qua community. How does Paul understand the reality of this community which is the body of Christ? Some of these characteristics are but corporate expressions of the individual, which we discussed in the preceding chapter. I will summarize these before moving to a description of some specifically corporate dimensions of the eschatological community.

First, within the community the joyous feelings of liberation were shared. In the worship meetings there was an intensity

2. See Robin Scroggs, "Paul as Rhetorician: Two Homilies in Romans 1–11," *Jews, Greeks, and Christians: Religious Cultures in Late Antiquity*, ed. R. Hamerton-Kelly and Robin Scroggs (Leiden, 1976).

foreign to most modern services. Glossolalia was apparently common, an expression which could and did on occasion get out of hand. But there were also prayer and prophecy and singing. There were agape meals, during which both food and joy were the key ingredients.

Second, the prominence of the reciprocal pronoun again calls for our attention. A few examples: "Love one another with brotherly affection" (Rom. 12:10). "Live in harmony with one another" (Rom. 12:16). "Outdo one another in showing honor" (Rom. 12:10). "May the God of steadfastness and encouragement grant you to agree with one another, in accord with Christ Jesus" (Rom. 15:5). "Let us no more pass judgment on one another" (Rom. 14:13). "Let us pursue what makes for peace and for mutual upbuilding" (Rom. 14:19). "Welcome one another, therefore, as Christ has welcomed you" (Rom. 15:7). "I myself am satisfied about you, my brethren, that you yourselves are full of goodness, filled with all knowledge, and able to instruct one another" (Rom. 15:14). "Greet one another with a holy kiss" (Rom. 16:16). All of these from the letter to the Romans alone! Clearly the reciprocal pronoun is a key word for Paul. The community is one of mutual sharing in all dimensions of its life. Peace, joy, and love come into full existence only in this mutual sharing.

Third, implied in the reciprocity of relationship is the equality of persons within the eschatological community. Paul accepts the obvious, that believers have different talents and capacities. There are the weak and the strong, the variously distributed gifts of the Spirit; there are male and female, Jew, Greek, slave, free. But his central theme, God's sheer gift of life for impious, that is, aggressive humanity, leads to the inescapable conclusion that before God all people are equal, and that means that this equality must be realized and expressed within the eschatological community. Societal or economic status is now irrelevant. Paul virtually ignores church hierarchy.[3] The community is to handle problems either as a committee of the whole or by individual members acting out of their own wisdom. (This says

---

3. He mentions bishops and deacons only once, in the salutation to the Philippians; and in 1 Thessalonians he encourages the church to respect those who are the leaders (no titles being named).

nothing about the necessity of church leaders today, as far as the
need for order and execution is concerned.) Paul acknowledges
the *distinctions* among people; he completely rejects any *value
judgments* derived from these distinctions.

Paul, further, acknowledges the validity of what we would call
roles in society, but he is sensitive to the ease by which a role
becomes an instrument of aggression and domination. One's
position of authority can function on the one hand as a means of
securing the self and on the other as a way of controlling and
manipulating others. Thus in Paul's churches roles play a very
minor part and are reduced to mere functions—sometimes someone can function as a prophet or teacher or healer.

In Galatians 3:27–28 Paul writes that very famous passage,
"For as many of you as were baptized into Christ have put on
Christ. There is neither Jew nor Greek, there is neither slave
nor free, there is neither male nor female; for you are all one in
Christ Jesus." Recent research has suggested that here Paul is
not freely composing but is citing in part an early Christian
baptismal formula.[4] This formula, then, reveals a basic insight
into the meaning of baptism for the Pauline churches. As one
leaves the old world, a world in which separation and domination are essential, and enters the new, the old hierarchical values
based on the differences in people are left behind. Within the
eschatological community, people, no matter of what background, shape, or form, are seen and accepted as equals. While
the three pairs in the passage point to only three of the greatest
separations and sources of inequality in the ancient world, it is
legitimate to broaden the perspective and to suggest that the
formula implies that *all* superior-inferior relationships are destroyed in the body of Christ.

Paul, of course, spent much of his life as a Christian apostle
fighting the divisions between Jew and Greek; I need say no
more about that. Within the church there were many slaves.
And it is almost certain (though we have no proof) that the
master of the slave, if he or she were a Christian, would frequently be 'a member of the same congregation. Within that

4. See Robin Scroggs, "Paul and the Eschatological Woman," *Journal of the
American Academy of Religion* 40 (1972): 291–92, and W. Meeks, "The Image
of the Androgyne: Some Uses of a Symbol in Earliest Christianity," *History
of Religions* 13 (1974): 180–82.

community the slave would participate on an equal footing with the master. Neither the church nor any other group in the ancient world mounted a protest against slavery as a system; nevertheless, within the church, slave and master were seen as equals. In 1 Corinthians 7 Paul suggests that slaves should not make great efforts to obtain their freedom, and then adds a curiously awkward phrase which could be interpreted either as suggesting that the slave *should* accept freedom if it became possible, or, quite to the contrary, that the possibility should *not* be actualized (1 Cor. 7:21).

That the former is the likely interpretation is suggested, I think, by that very winning and subtle letter of Paul to Philemon. You will recall that a runaway slave of Philemon named Onesimus has sought out Paul in prison. Paul talks him into returning to his master accompanied by the letter. While the letter does not *command* Philemon to release Onesimus, it takes little reading between the lines to become aware that this is the purpose of the writing. The request is made even bolder by the hint that Onesimus stole from Philemon as he escaped. Whether Paul stood for emancipation of slaves or not, the baptismal formula speaks of the elimination of dominance "in Christ," and that means within the church itself, its meetings, its fellowship.

It is commonly thought, however, that Paul's views on the equality of male and female were quite different. He has even been labeled an extreme male chauvinist. If this is true, it is a blatant denial of the basic theological premise on which everything in his theology is based. This alone should at least make us open to a reassessment of the general assumptions. Here I can only state in brief form what I have tried to substantiate in more detail elsewhere.[5]

(1) The authentic Paul must be separated from the pseudo-Paul. Whatever is said in Ephesians, Colossians, and the Pastorals cannot be used to create a picture of Paul's views toward women.[6] All the demonstrably chauvinist passages usually quoted against Paul are in this secondary literature, with one exception.

5. See the previous note and Robin Scroggs, "Paul and the Eschatological Woman: Revisited," *Journal of the American Academy of Religion* 42 (1974): 532–37.

6. See ch. 1, note 2.

(2) The one exception is 1 Corinthians 14:33b–36, where women are admonished to keep silent in church meetings. They are not even to ask questions. For several reasons scholars have considered for years the possibility that this passage is a later, non-Pauline insertion into the original letter. Chief of these is that it blatantly contradicts what Paul has just finished saying in 1 Corinthians 11; women, he clearly states, not only can ask questions but also can preach and pray publicly. People unfamiliar with biblical scholarship may tend to find such a claim of secondary insertion a specious way to protect an argument. Secondary insertions are, however, quite common in the literature of the New Testament and to scholars they are an everyday matter.

(3) In the various lists of greetings found in the Pauline corpus, a number of women are named who are workers and leaders in the church. For example, in Philippians he writes, "I entreat Euodia and I entreat Syntyche to agree in the Lord. And I ask you also, true yokefellow, help these women, for they have labored side by side with me in the gospel together with Clement and the rest of my fellow workers, whose names are in the book of life" (Phil. 4:2–3). Nothing is said to distinguish the kind of work they are doing from that of men. Since there is absolutely nothing in the texts which would suggest a subordination of roles, Paul must have accepted them as equal to male leaders.

(4) Only two authentic Pauline passages can possibly be the grounds for claiming Paul to be a chauvinist. The first is 1 Corinthians 7. Here Paul is answering questions put to him by, apparently, an ascetic group in the church. I think it is without question that in this section Paul (a) affirms the legitimacy of marriage, (b) affirms the legitimacy of sexuality within marriage, (c) makes it clear that men and women have equal rights and responsibilities within sex and marriage, and (d) prefers the single state only because he opts for the extended family of the church over against the nuclear family, as I argued in chapter 2.

(5) The second questionable passage is 1 Corinthians 11:2–16. Here Paul argues vehemently that women when leading worship (praying and prophesying) should wear a head-covering. This is an extremely difficult text, not only—I would say not

even primarily—because in the way it is usually read it seems to put women down, but also (and primarily) because the passage as a whole is opaque. We just do not have the information to put together a coherent and ultimately satisfying interpretation of the whole. But what is most crucially important is clear. Paul in no way tries to inhibit the right of women to be worship leaders. He does insist that they should wear something on their heads when they do pray or preach, while he is equally insistent that men should not. If the issue had been Corinthian men wanting to wear a head covering, Paul would, apparently, have attacked that practice. He is trying, almost desperately, to maintain *distinctions* between the sexes, yet he equally refuses to place valuations on those distinctions. I have suggested elsewhere that the hidden agenda in Paul at this point might be his fear of homosexuality. I am more convinced than ever that this is correct, although it is obviously incapable of proof.

The issue of subordination seems to emerge in v. 3, where Christ is said to be the *kephale* (head) of men, and men to be the *kephale* of women. "But I want you to understand that the head of every man is Christ, the head of a woman is her husband, and the head of Christ is God." Obviously a metaphorical meaning is intended for the word *head*, but which metaphorical meaning is the correct one? The word is ordinarily understood here to mean *ruler* or *authority*, as is idiomatic to Hebrew and English. In Greek, however, the word *head* does *not* normally have that idiomatic meaning. A common Greek metaphorical use of *kephale*, however, would be to denote a *source*, and it is this meaning which fits v. 3. Christ is the *source* of man (the motif of Christ as creator) and man is the *source* of woman (Gen. 2). I submit that it should be taken here in its ordinary Greek metaphorical meaning.

If this is correct, Paul seems to be playing on a Christian interpretation of Genesis 2. Here, you recall, God creates Adam, and from Adam Eve is created. From the Christian point of view, God is the source of all life; from God comes the preexistent Christ, who is the agent of creation; as agent Christ then creates Adam (here we are back to the Genesis text); and from Adam comes Eve. It is constructive to see that a Greek father of the church, Cyril of Alexandria, interpreted the passage in precisely this manner. "Thus we say that the head of every man is Christ, because he was excellently made through him. And the head of woman is man, because she was taken from his flesh. Likewise, the head of Christ is God, because he is from Him according to nature."[7]

I believe that from these arguments it can be legitimately concluded that Paul supported the equality of male and female in the church just as certainly as he did that of Jew and Greek, slave and free. Thus his working out of relationships in the church is consistent with his theology of liberation and equality of all persons before the gracious God who gives life.

The post-Pauline period, and even those anonymous folk who wrote in his name, betrayed these views of egalitarianism, because they no longer had the courage or insight to live out of the basic rubric of justification by grace. And while it is not our purpose to follow this betrayal, it is instructive to look at one specific facet of the later literature. In the post-Pauline writings using his name there emerges a particular form of ethical admonition, which is apparently borrowed from the larger Greek culture and thus is not created by Christians themselves. This form describes the proper relationships within the family (a family wealthy enough to include slaves). In this form the relationships are without exception structured according to domination/ subjection. Husbands are to dominate their wives; parents, their children; masters, their slaves. This form is called by scholars the "household tables."[8] Adoption by late first-century Christianity of these tables laid the death knell to the egalitarianism lived by the earlier church, and it is only in such passages that the subordination of women to men is explicitly stated in the entire New Testament. Now the interesting observation to make regarding Paul is this: since this form was at hand in the larger Greek culture, Paul must surely have known of it. Yet he

---

7. G.W.H. Lampe, ed. *A Patristic Greek Lexicon*, s.v., (New York: Oxford University Press, 1961–1968), p. 749.

8. The main passages are Colossians 3:18–4:1, and Ephesians 5:21–6:9; also see 1 Timothy 2:8–15. A similar form also appears in the New Testament in 1 Peter 2:13–3:7. A careful reading of the passage in Ephesians is, however, instructive. The model for the husband of the self-giving of Christ has virtually reduced any domination of male over female.

never uses it. Is this an accident, or is it a deliberate act, neces-
sitated because he is aware that the structure itself is false to his
basic theology of justification by grace?

The fourth and last of the characteristics of the eschatological
community which are corporate expressions of the individual has
to do with the most popular term for the church in Paul, the
body of Christ. But I think it fair to say that the term has been
made popular by theologians and exegetes more so than by Paul
himself. The full term *body of Christ* appears actually only once
in the genuine Pauline corpus, and Paul has only one extended
discussion of the motif, which may have developed simply out of
an ad hoc comparison, or analogy. This occurs in 1 Corinthians
12. Paul does return to the motif in Romans, but only in passing.[9] It was not a key motif for him, but I mention it at this
point because it has a function in relation to the egalitarian
nature of the church, which we have just been discussing.

In 1 Corinthians the motif emerges within a large discussion of
the so-called spiritual gifts. The background seems to be that
some Corinthians were fluent in speaking in tongues and claimed
that this was the spiritual gift par excellence, that gift which
showed they were closest to God and thus were supreme in the
kingdom of God. Paul sees that they are using a gift given by
God (thus by grace) to grasp after their own security (thus falsi-
fying the gift into justification by works) and to create an elitist
theology precisely out of that gift which *destroys* every elitist
position. Little wonder that Paul is firm in his rejection of this
elitist position.

His first attack is to deal with the issue in the terms the Corinthians were accustomed to, in terms of the spiritual gifts. His
argument is that while the gifts themselves vary, each gift comes
from the same Spirit of God and the decision as to which gift a
person will receive is not the person's but God's. Furthermore,
these gifts are not for the individual's benefit and prideful self-
esteem, but for the community. In a sentence so typical of Paul's
reflexes he writes, "To each is given the manifestation of the
Spirit for the common good" (1 Cor. 12:7).

9. Romans 12:3–8. He does say in 1 Corinthians 6:15, "Do you not know that
your bodies are members of Christ?" The context there is, however, somewhat
different, and thus the function of the metaphor is different.

It is at this point that he picks up the analogy of the body, because it gives him the same opportunity to speak of the whole and the parts. The body is a wholistically functioning organism which is nevertheless made up of various parts, each with its own function, a function which contributes to the life of the organism as a whole. And since the organism is a unity and a totality, one cannot really say, so the argument runs, that one part is more essential or important than another. Furthermore, since the organism *is* a totality, what happens to one organ affects all others in that totality. If I break my leg, it is my leg that is broken; yet the pain and other inconveniences affect my total self. Paul summarizes his point, still using his analogy but obviously thinking about the problem in the church. The purpose of God's creating the body the way he has is "that there be no schism in the body, but that the members may have the same care for one another. If one member suffers, all suffer together; if one member is honored, all rejoice together" (1 Cor. 12:25–26). The notion of a schism in a physical body is a jolting idea, and the RSV more smoothly translates it as *discord*. The Greek word Paul uses here, however, *is* the word *schism*, and is precisely that word which he uses at the beginning of the letter to speak of the partylike divisions within the church (1 Cor. 1:10). His double entendre must have spoken clearly to the Corinthians; since the *source* of the gifts is God and since the *purpose* of the gifts is the common good, any division upon which value judgments are made about persons is a betrayal of God's act of justification in Christ.

Thus the *function* of the analogy in 1 Corinthians is not to set out some ontology of the church, not primarily to relate the church to Christ in some mystical union, but rather to use the church as a weapon in fighting the misuse, the betrayal, of God's act in Christ. *The worst sin of all is to create an elitism out of precisely that act which eliminates any possibility of elitism.* The analogy of the body is important, but it should, perhaps, assume a more modest place—at least a different one—from that which it frequently is given in our handbooks of Pauline theology.

SEPARATION BETWEEN CHURCH AND WORLD

Paul thus describes a reality within the community completely different from that of the world of sin and death. This raises for us a crucial question. If the two worlds are so radically different, and if Berger and Luckmann are correct in saying that a new world needs to protect itself by cutting itself off from the old world, we should expect a strongly sectarian separation to appear in the Pauline churches. The expectation does not materialize, however, in any clear fashion. The issue in fact is extremely complex, since Paul's dialectical theology is complex. The issue of separation from and participation in the world is, however, crucial. We must therefore attend to the data with some care.

The separation. The basic stance of Paul must be carefully expressed. Paul believes the *reality* of the new creation must be kept separated from contamination by the *reality* of the world of sin and death. That means, first and foremost, that Paul is *not* after the separation of people, of one group of people from another. He believes that a certain quality of existence is to be realized within the communities, and it is this quality he strives to keep pure.

If a member fails to live that quality, Paul exhorts others to "restore him in a spirit of gentleness" (Gal. 6:1). This gentleness, however, does not always work. For example, Paul is confronted with an extreme case in the Corinthian community. A believer is either married to or living with the former wife of his father (*not* his own mother). While the woman is thus not of blood relation, the cohabitation is prohibited both by the Old Testament and by Roman law. Since nothing is said about repentance and change on the part of the brother, it would seem that he has been counseled about the irregularity of the matter and has refused to leave his beloved. The Corinthian church has taken no further action against the person.

Paul has no doubt in his mind about what ought to be done. "Let him who has done this be removed from among you" (1 Cor. 5:2). "You are to deliver this man to Satan for the destruction of the flesh, that the spirit may be saved in the day of the Lord Jesus" (1 Cor. 5:5). "Do you not know that a little leaven leavens the whole lump? Cleanse out the old leaven that you may be a new lump" (1 Cor. 5:6–7). The difficulties in this passage are notorious, and we cannot stop to consider them. What *is* clear is that here we have Paul at his strictest, most unyielding, apparently least compassionate self. Without attempting to defend the Apostle, I do think the reason for his attitude is reasonably clear. He is concerned that the community be kept in its purity. The image of the leaven cited above suggests this in emphatic fashion. The images Paul uses elsewhere for the church—the temple of God, the Spirit, the body of Christ—all suggest the same drive toward purity.

In fact, later in the same chapter Paul makes a peculiar distinction that is intelligible only if what he is primarily protecting is the purity of the community. "I wrote to you in my letter not to associate with immoral men; not at all meaning the immoral of this world, or the greedy and robbers, or idolators, since then you would need to go out of the world" (1 Cor. 5:9–10). He then explains that what he meant to say in this previous letter was that they should not associate with a *Christian* who lived in an immoral fashion. He does not ask the community to withdraw from the secular world; he does not even seem to ask them to be particular about what sort of pagans they associate with. The implication is that it is expected that one deals with, works with, "immoral" people in the world.

Yet that quality of existence which one encounters in the old world is not to be permitted in the eschatological community which lives out of the new. Thus a careful distinction and separation in the quality of existence is insisted upon. What exists outside the church must not be permitted to enter it. Thus there is a separation, but not of the usual kind. The church is not prohibited from entering the world; the world is excluded from entering the church.

The participation. As in all dialectic there is another side to the issue. Paul acknowledges the legitimacy and sometimes the necessity of living and participating in secular reality.

As far as the world of *things* is concerned, Paul has no uneasiness at all. We have already seen that Paul has no qualms about eating meat which has been sacrificed to pagan gods. Nor does he any longer think certain foods ritually unclean. "I know and am persuaded in the Lord Jesus that nothing is unclean in itself" (Rom. 14:14). This verse lays down an antipietistic, world-accepting program that could and did carry over into areas other than that concerning food. And when he counsels, "Let . . . those who deal with the world [live] as though they had no dealings with it" (1 Cor. 7:31), he is not suggesting a stoic withdrawal from the world but warning against making participation in the secular world an ultimate concern.

The Apostle's judgment about mixed marriages (between believer and nonbeliever) is typical of the way in which he makes decisions vis-à-vis believer and world. Some Corinthians have, apparently, raised the separationist question, Should believers divorce their unbelieving spouses? (1 Cor. 7:10–16). That is, should the family be made to be entirely within the community? Paul's answer, to begin with, is *no*. The believer should want the marriage to continue. But the believer cannot dictate to the spouse; in fact, he or she must allow the nonbeliever to make the decision. If the nonbeliever consents to the continuation of the marriage, it should continue. If the nonbeliever wishes dissolution, the couple should divorce. Here it is clear that Paul's general ethical maxim, that one should put himself or herself in the service of the other, holds for people outside the community as well as those inside.

But more is involved. While Paul apparently knows of Jesus' word about the indissolubility of marriage (Mark 10:2–12) and takes it as important, he does not hold to this rigidly. The key consideration is the quality of the marriage. In the case of dissension within mixed marriages over the religious issue (which is apparently what the problem is), divorce is acceptable when asked for by the pagan spouse, because the marriage has lost its basic and essential quality of *peace*. "For God has called us to peace" (1 Cor. 7:15).

For better or worse we cannot avoid in this discussion the famous, or infamous, passage in Romans 13:1–7, where Paul legitimizes the payment of taxes and general obedience to the Roman empire. It is infamous in a political sense because it has been used to create a Christian quietism in the face of demonic and oppressive governments. It is infamous in an exegetical sense because it is extremely difficult to harmonize some of the things Paul says here with what he suggests elsewhere. This has led some scholars to the point of questioning its authenticity. Perhaps it is a later insertion into the genuine Pauline letter.

On the assumption, however, that it is genuine, we have to admit that Paul says two very clear things. The first is that the believer is responsible for participation in the ongoing process of the civil government. Most Christians of Paul's day belonged to the lower classes and thus were shut out from personal participation in the governmental structures. The only way they could participate would be through the payment of taxes and other revenues required by the Roman government. Thus what Paul says here is consonant with what he says elsewhere about legitimate and responsible participation in secular society.

The second affirmation is the warrant he gives for this participation: governments have their authority only from God and are thus divinely ordained. Charges of inconsistency are unavoidable at this point. Elsewhere Paul makes it clear that the world outside the eschatological community is not under the control of God but of demonic powers and principalities, or Satan.[10] And surely the state, although in Paul's day it was in general a responsible and reasonably unoppressive government, must belong to the unredeemed world and also be under the control of the demonic powers. If the passage is authentic, I think we have to admit that Paul is simply inconsistent. At the most we can make a distinction between the *conduct* urged by Paul and the politicotheological *warrants* which buttress his ethical exhortation. While the warrant is inconsistent with what Paul says elsewhere, the conduct urged displays Paul's general perspective that the believer is responsible for God's world, whether or not that part of the world in question acknowledges the true God.

Paul's judgments are thus hardly simplistic but yet are basically clear and self-consistent. The church must be kept pure and worldly reality prohibited from contaminating the eschatological community based on justification by faith. Yet

---

10. Paul shared this view of the rule over the world by invisible demonic powers with both Jews and Greeks. See 1 Corinthians 15:24–25; Romans 8:38–39; 2 Corinthians 4:4; Galatians 4:8–9.

the individual believer is free to participate in responsible action toward the world. And notice that none of these instances involve questions about missionary, that is, explicitly religious activity, although it goes without saying that Paul and his churches did missionize among the unbelievers. The gamut runs from joyous feasts to mixed marriages to governmental taxes—thus secular matters are the issues raised.

I think this may say something to the church's perplexity about where to stand in its self-understanding vis-à-vis the outside world. Is it to be a church which exists for itself, attending to, eliciting, and celebrating that eschatological reality found within its walls? Or is it to be a community which breaks down the walls and participates in the social realities and problems of the world outside? Should it be involved in the social gospel? In one sense, Paul has no answer to the latter; neither in Paul, the church at large, nor any other congregation, religious, philosophical, or otherwise, of Paul's day were there such things as social protests and activist assaults upon the injustices of society. Yet the implications are, I believe, there. Paul *did* encourage participation in the world, and by extension I believe he would, if alive today, have been in the front of protest marches against racism and the war in Vietnam.

Thus the answer Paul gives to these questions is that both the church as attending to its own unique and joyous existence *and* the church as an arm of God in the world are legitimate and indeed necessary. There is no conflict necessary between these models. In fact, I would suggest that that church which really celebrates within itself the restoration to authentic personhood is *necessarily* going to move into the world. Equally clearly, the church involved in social protest cannot continue to exist for long unless it participates in the joyous life of justification by faith. The split in our churches over this issue seems to me doubly tragic because it is a false and unnecessary split.

CONCLUSION

I would like to sum up by drawing out what seems to me a very important implication of what we have been considering. It is very clear that Paul believes a reality exists in the eschatological community which is different from that in the world. He affirms that this eschatological reality is better, truer, more authentic for human existence than that reality lived by the culture of sin and death. Furthermore it is clear that Paul wants carefully to maintain that reality within the community and is prepared, when necessary, to take rather extreme steps to do so. In short, he thinks Christians have access to something the world does not.

At the same time he destroys the grounds for any sort of elitism. Since life is sheer gift, no one earns it, and the only boast can be in God (1 Cor. 1:31). Nor would Paul accept an egalitarianism inside but an elitism of the insiders over against the outsiders. He affirms the reality inside. He emphatically rejects judgment of people outside. "For what have I to do with judging outsiders? . . . God judges those outside" (1 Cor. 5:12–13).

Paul's dialectical theology has again led him to walk a fine line between two unacceptable extremes, the one of blurring the distinction between Christian reality and worldly reality, and the other of creating a Christian elitism. Very few of our churches today walk this fine line. The liberal churches have fallen into the trap of blurring the distinction; the evangelical churches have tended to fall into the opposite error, that of Christian elitism, or what might be called Christian imperialism. Each church is fearfully aware of the trap the other has fallen into, without adequately tending to its own imprisonment. But if the church could live with Paul under the banner of justification by grace in faith, then the danger of elitism could be avoided and that new reality of eschatological community could still be experienced, celebrated, and enjoyed.

Ethics:
Eschatological Action[1]

The discussion in our brief study has so far centered on "being" rather than "doing." A few hints have been dropped about action, but it may seem as if I have deliberately avoided addressing what for so many folk is the most important thing: "But what should I do?" Such perception would be correct, for I have tried hard *not* to talk about works, about the activity of morality, precisely because our history of American pragmatic Christianity has so often foreclosed almost all interest in other kinds of theological discussion. Somehow "being" seems abstract and unrelated to actual living; it is only when we are "doing" that life becomes meaningful and worthwhile. I think it is clear to us all that the American church has often succumbed to a theology of justification by works. Were Paul to appear to us today, would he be any less indignant about our life than he was in the first century? Unfortunately our sometimes frantic activism may impede our understanding, even, of the depths of Paul's theology of grace.

Nevertheless, no one can doubt that Paul was himself an activist. As a Jew, he was fanatic; as a Christian, frenetic. The Book of Acts gives us almost a misleading portrait of early Christian missionary activity, as if the gospel were spread in the West only by Paul and his disciples. This, of course, is false, and is an impression no doubt not intended by its author, who could count

1. For an extremely informative book covering the scope of this chapter the reader is encouraged to consult V. P. Furnish, *Theology and Ethics in Paul* (Nashville: Abingdon, 1968).

on his readers to supply their own list of known and honored missionaries. Certainly, though, Paul could hardly have been surpassed in his energy, his unceasing concern, and his total devotion to the missionary enterprise.

Without question Paul also expected from people in his churches a high ethical performance. What we call "ethics" was no secondary concern for him, and it is now time to center on this concern. But we must again be prepared for surprises. If he sees life as gift rather than as won by activism, then we should expect his ethical program to be significantly different from all those, Christian, Jewish, or otherwise, which essentially are based on justification by works. This theological grounding determines the structure of this chapter. First we must seek to find his understanding of the relation between being and doing. Only after that is accomplished can we inspect some specific ethical guidelines which he considers important.

THE THEOLOGICAL BASIS FOR ACTION

Justification by grace means that one is saved *before*, or prior to, ethical acts, not as a result of such acts. From all we have said, this is obvious by now. But someone usually manages to ask the question, "But if that is so, why *should* I do good deeds?" That question is very revealing. It suggests that one would not act unless there was something in it for the actor. Need I say that the question itself presupposes a posture of justification by works, based on that lack of being which can only use other people in the project of securing the self? The ethical act that stems from justification by grace is totally different. It is spontaneous, truly directed toward the other out of concern for the other.

The above means that *any* set of rules can be only a guideline for action; it can never be a criterion for salvation. This statement must be taken in absolute starkness. The Ten Commandments, other ethical rules in the Old Testament, and *even the teaching of Jesus in the Gospels* cannot become for the believer the criterion by which his or her salvation or damnation is measured. Lest this be thought some modern heresy, I shall quote

Thomas Aquinas. He is explaining 2 Corinthians 3:6: "For the letter kills, but the Spirit gives life." By "letter" Paul is clearly referring to the precepts of the Old Testament, but Aquinas generalizes: "The letter denotes any writing that is external to man, even that of the moral precepts such as are contained in the Gospel. Wherefore the letter, even of the Gospel, would kill, unless there were the inward presence of the healing grace of faith."[2] Paul cites few sayings of Jesus in his letters. Could the reason have been that he was afraid people would start considering them law necessary for salvation (as had already begun to happen before the first century was over)?

We have already seen that living under the banner of justification by grace frees one actually to be able to love for the first time. But there is another key dimension of adequate ethical activity, and that is *knowledge*. I may *wish* to help, but I must also know *how* to help. Even more basically I must be free to know that my help is needed. Only existence in faith can provide such awareness or knowledge. Depth knowledge, after all, is not simply or primarily facts or accumulation of data. Knowledge with regard to ethical action is first of all *accurate perception* of the reality of the other and the various needs being expressed in any given situation. Anxiety about the self can only produce a distorted sense of the external world. I am not truly interested in the other, but only in using the other to secure myself, and thus I do not genuinely perceive the other. Only the self-forgetfulness of faith enables me to know the other and his or her cry for help. Of course I need data; of course I need training, to know how best to help. But data and training are impotent to remove the blinders of anxiety from persons' eyes.

Thus there is a *noetic* transformation in persons coming to faith in the God who gives, a transformation which, because freeing persons to love, enables them to have a firmer and more knowledgeable basis upon which to act. The psychologist Abraham Maslow has developed an understanding of mature, fulfilled love which he calls "being-love" (or "B-love," for short), and he

2. Thomas Aquinas, *Summa Theologica* (New York: McGraw-Hill, 1970), vol. 2, part 1, q. 106, a. 2.

also is aware of its noetic implications. "The truest, most pene-
trating perception of the other is made possible by B-love. It is
as much a cognitive as an emotional-conative reaction. . . . Far
from accepting the common platitude that love makes people
blind, I become more and more inclined to think of the *opposite*
as true, namely that non-love makes us blind."[3]

Paul, I believe, is aware in general of the new perceptions of
reality brought him through justification by grace. He has rethought his whole theology, his whole understanding of the relation between God and humanity, and his whole reading of the
history of Israel. In one sentence he suggests he is also aware of
how this noetic transformation influenced ethical conduct and
judgment. "And it is my prayer that your love *may constantly
increase in knowledge and all moral insight,* so that you may test
what is excellent and may be pure and blameless for the day of
Christ" (Phil. 1:9–10; italics mine). Freedom to love, based on
justification by grace, leads to moral insight.

Paul states this relationship beautifully in his introduction to
the section on ethical admonitions in Romans. "I appeal to you
therefore brethren, by the mercies of God, to present your bodies
as a living sacrifice, holy and acceptable to God, which is your
spiritual [or more literally, rational] worship. Do not be con-
formed to this world, but be transformed by the renewal of your
mind, that you may prove [that is, test out] what is the will of
God, what is good and acceptable and perfect" (Rom. 12:1–2).
Here the "new being" has as a component a "new mind," a new
rationality, which has the capacity to search out what is the will
of God. The Greek word here translated *renewal* could almost
be taken in the sense of "restoration." It is a mind restored to
that clear rationality which God always intended persons to
have, so that they might be able to search out his will.

Just as in everything else, Paul ties action to the *eschaton.*
The believer's act is an eschatological act. He expresses this by
claiming the believer's ethical activity to be the result of the
power of the Spirit of God. We have said far too little so far
about the Spirit, unavoidably perhaps; but it is equally unavoid-

3. Abraham Maslow, *Toward a Psychology of Being* (New York: Van Nostrand,
1968), p. 41.

able *not* to raise the subject when Pauline ethic is being discussed.

Early Christians in general celebrated the presence of God's Spirit in the church as the inbreaking of the kingdom. But what kind of activities were thought of as provoked and sustained by the Spirit? Primarily, it seems, the earliest church was guided by Old Testament notions of the Spirit of God as being that power which invaded people, giving them temporarily more than human abilities in this activity or that. In the early church the Spirit was associated with the more-than-normal: miracles, prophecies, healing, speaking in tongues, interpreting the meaning of those who spoke in tongues. These were no doubt seen as helping and helpful activities, but they were all extraordinary kinds of activities, all something above mundane, everyday life.

None of this Paul denies. He was himself an ecstatic and mystic. What Paul does do, and insofar as we have data available was the first to do, is to broaden understanding of the activity of the Spirit to cover all the everyday, *ethical* acts of the believer. Not only the religious heroes have a right to claim the Spirit of God; the ordinary believer, without spiritual powers in the old sense, has now an equal confidence that God's Spirit is with and in him or her, guiding his or her life. In fact, Paul states the matter in the most extreme terms. In the Corinthian dispute about the importance of this versus that spiritual gift, Paul accepts the validity of these powerful acts. Yet in the midst of the discussion, he suddenly says, "And I will show you a still more excellent way" (1 Cor. 12:14b). And what follows this sentence? We all know: his hymn to love. Even the humblest believer, without any of those spiritual gifts so boasted about by some of the Corinthians, can be bigger than any of them, when love spontaneously bursts forth from his or her existence. Nor should we forget that when Paul describes the virtues of the Christian life in Galatians, he calls them the "fruit of the Spirit."

Since Paul knows that action flows out of being, he *expects* righteous living from his congregations. This may sound rather obvious, particularly when certain passages of Paul are quoted, such as this one: "Do you not know that the unrighteous will not inherit the kingdom of God? Do not be deceived; neither the

immoral, nor idolaters, nor adulterers, nor catamites, nor ped-
erasts,[4] nor thieves, nor the greedy, nor drunkards, nor revilers,
nor robbers will inherit the kingdom of God" (1 Cor. 6:9–10).
Yet this raises a question about our central theme, that persons
are *not* justified by ethical actions. If, furthermore, one wishes
to claim that Paul's phrase "justification of the impious" (Rom.
4:5) refers to a permanent condition of the person before God,
even the Christian person, the question becomes insistently
pertinent. The burden of this chapter is to reject that phrase as
directly applicable to the *Christian* person, but such interpretation of its applicability has a long history in Christian theology.
Indeed, some scholars have been so disturbed by the apparent
conflict between Paul's emphasis upon justification by grace and
the sometimes strict ethical admonitions that they have concluded that Paul was basically inconsistent. He was drawing
from two separate theological systems but was never able to in-
tegrate and harmonize them.

I can appreciate the frustrations of those who reach this des-
perate conclusion, but first it seems to me incumbent upon the
interpreter to make sense of the tension in Paul, to seek as long
as possible for a solution which saves the integrity of the Apostle's thinking. Not that we are out to "save" Paul; it is rather
that, everything being equal, such a solution is more likely to be
accurate.

---

4. Since the issue of homosexuality is currently so debated in the church, it
is imperative to be as precise as possible about what Paul does and does not
say about it. Only twice does he mention the practice, once in Romans 1:26–27,
where he seems indebted to stock Hellenistic-Jewish proclamation, and in the
list in 1 Corinthians 6:9. Here two words are pertinent, and it is unfortunate
that the RSV loosely uses one word, *homosexuals*, to cover both terms. The
first word, *malakos*, literally means "soft," and from the literal meaning is
derived its metaphorical sense, "effeminate." There is some evidence that the
word could also point to the practice of the catamite. The catamite was a
youth who had been trained to receive the advances (which were not always
only sexual) of an adult male. While the catamite could come from a free and
wealthy family, the practice also could involve prostitution and slavery (cf.
Robert Flacellière, *Love in Ancient Greece* [New York: Macfadden, 1962],
pp. 81–84).
The second word, *arsenokoitēs*, must then refer to the adult male who uses
the catamite. Thus what Paul is attacking here is not homosexuality in general but a specific custom which at best was characterized by lust and at worst
could degenerate into the inhuman dimensions of prostitution and slavery. I
am not suggesting that Paul would have accepted a homosexual relationship
between mature adults, but I do think it important to keep in mind just what
actual practices Paul opposed.

Let me suggest the following as a possible perspective. I have said that God's act of justification is not simply an act of forgiveness. It is rather a creative act which frees the person from inauthentic life to enable that person to live in his or her full creatureliness. Part of the description of that new person is precisely that he or she is now free to act for others, to mold his or her life according to God's intent for humanity. The incentive for acting is now no longer a striving for salvation; it is a spontaneous act of love for the sake not of self but of the other.

Thus the ethical act flows out of the *being* justified by grace and is not separate from that being; it is an indivisible part of a seamless garment. To change the metaphor, it is that part of the iceberg which is visible above the surface of the water but which is just part of a reality that extends far below. For Paul, sinful deeds reveal that the person is not living, at that moment, in faith toward the God who gives life.

This is not to suggest that Paul is merely affirming that the subjective below-the-surface iceberg is the only thing that is important, so that the sinful deeds eliminate one from the kingdom of God simply because they reveal the inadequacy of the subjective. That would again separate faith from deed, and for Paul faith/deed is all one human, eschatological reality. The deed is an essential part of that new creation based on justification by grace.

Is Paul then inconsistent when he says that people who sin will not enter the kingdom of God? As far as I can think through the matter, I do not believe that he is, although Paul's dialectic forces him again to sail a narrow passage between Scylla and Charybdis. Ethical expectations do not nullify the claim that life is gift. They rather are descriptions of what that gifted life looks like. That is perhaps the best way to put it. Paul's ethical exhortations are *descriptions*, not *prescriptions*.

NORMS FOR PAULINE ETHICS

A second kind of question must be raised, the answer to which will lead us in the same direction. When Paul does suggest ethical actions, does he appeal to some norm external to his own insight? The answer leads us first to some negative statements.

The norm is not the Old Testament. Paul uses the Old Testament frequently in the theological portions of his letters.
When he turns to ethical exhortations, such references become
less frequent and less explicit. When they do appear, they are
usually subtly interwoven into a basically non-Old Testament
context. For example, while treating the theme of peaceful existence among people, he suddenly inserts this passage from Prov-
erbs: "If your enemy is hungry, feed him; if he is thirsty, give
him drink; for by so doing you will heap burning coals on his
head" (Rom. 12:20, quoting Prov. 25:21–22). Presumably Paul
knew what he thought that passage meant; we don't.

He appeals to the ethical part of the Ten Commandments only
to say that they are fulfilled in the logion from Leviticus, "You
shall love your neighbor as yourself" (but cf. the negative reference in Romans 2:20–24). Interestingly enough, neither of the
times he cites that passage does he mention that Jesus also
quoted it and made it the center of his ethic. Thus, in general,
ethical commands and prohibitions from the Old Testament are
infrequent, and while they *inform*, they do not *determine* his
basic ethical norm. There is no opportunity here to discuss the
influence of early Jewish ethics on Paul; the conclusion, however,
would be the same as for the Old Testament. Paul uses such
material, but it does not become his norm.

The norm is not the teaching of Jesus. Here especially, Paul
seems strangely silent, but the issue is complex. Sayings which
are *explicitly* said to be Jesus' sayings are rare. Paul knows
Jesus' saying on divorce (1 Cor. 7:10–11, cf. Mark 10:2–12). In
a discussion with the Corinthians about the right of missionaries
to be supported by church congregations, he writes, "In the same
way, the Lord commanded that those who proclaim the gospel
should get their living by the gospel" (1 Cor. 9:14). Presumably
this is a reference to the saying of Jesus, "The laborer deserves
his wages" (Luke 10:7; cf. Matt. 10:10). In Romans 14:14 he
says, "I know and am persuaded in the Lord Jesus that nothing is
unclean in itself." This *may* be dependent on Jesus' logion,
"There is nothing outside a person which by going into him can
defile him; but the things which come out of a person are what
defile him" (Mark 7:15). And, finally, he bases his apocalyptic

vision in 1 Thessalonians on the authority of Jesus: "For this we declare to you by the word of the Lord" (4:15). Unfortunately, the description which follows cannot be paralleled in any passage in our gospels; thus we do not know how much of that description was based on the Jesus tradition. These are the only passages in the entire Pauline corpus where he gives any explicit indication of appealing to the words of Jesus, apart from the nonethical pericope of the Lord's Supper (1 Cor. 11:23) and a doubtful reference in 1 Corinthians 14:37.

A number of scholars, however, appeal to a much larger group of passages in which they believe Paul is *alluding* to materials from the Jesus tradition. W. D. Davies, for instance, claims sixteen such instances from Romans and 1 Thessalonians, and in a carefully argued book, D. Dungan concludes that it may have been more characteristic of Paul to refer to the Jesus tradition in an allusive manner than in an explicit way.[5] The problem, of course, is how to establish that a passage *is* an allusive "citation." The similarity could be due to a general and common vocabulary within a community, perhaps borrowed in this case directly from Judaism. How close does the common vocabulary have to be before it counts? How do we know that Paul didn't say it first, since his letters precede the finalization of the gospels themselves? Thus the issue of the number of allusive "citations" is never likely to be solved to everyone's satisfaction.

I have no doubt but that some of the examples suggested by Davies are allusions to material that first appeared in the oral tradition about Jesus. But in my judgment, when all is said and done, the paucity of *explicit* citations used to guide ethical action speaks louder than any massive collection of suggested allusions.

Thus I believe Paul's ethic is *not* centrally based on the tradition of Jesus' teaching. Why more does not appear is difficult to answer, but it is all of a piece with the general silence of Paul about most of the traditions which will later make up the synoptic gospels. Some scholars have even suggested that Paul was not

5. William D. Davies, *Paul and Rabbinic Judaism: Some Rabbinic Elements in Pauline Theology* (New York: Harper & Row), pp. 136–40; D. Dungan, *The Sayings of Jesus in the Churches of Paul* (Philadelphia: Fortress Press, 1971), pp. 148–49; also the analysis in Furnish, *Theology and Ethics in Paul*, pp. 51–65.

very well acquainted with these traditions. I hypothesized above that Paul may have wanted to avoid the danger of someone turning Jesus' teaching into a new law. However that may be, the norm for Paul's ethic lies elsewhere.

The norm is not taken from Greek wisdom or religion. From this source he also draws up material occasionally, and his rhetorical style is heavily influenced by Greek models. Evidence of direct borrowing, however, is weak indeed. Frequently Paul lists series of vices and virtues as descriptions of behavior to be emulated or avoided. Scholars have labeled these *catalogues.* It is possible that Paul patterned his lists on Greek philosophical-religious forms, although recent scholarship has suggested the likelihood of Judaism as the direct predecessor of Paul's catalogues. The lists tend to be loosely strung together without much order or logic, and Paul uses them primarily as summaries of the general ethical product of the sinful or the justified person.

Most of the catalogues in Paul are of vices (e.g., Rom. 1:29–31; 1 Cor. 6:9–10; Gal. 5:19–21). The major list of virtues (Gal. 5:22–23) is so characteristically Pauline that I think it likely that Paul himself composed it, while those of the vices he probably took over from the stock of the wandering cynic or Jewish preacher. The catalogue, however, which seems closest to Greek ideas appears in Philippians 4:8: "Finally, brethren, whatever is lovely, whatever is gracious, if there is anything worthy of praise, think about these things." To say that these lists, as summaries, are descriptions rather than prescriptions is to state the obvious. The norm lies elsewhere.

The norm for Paul's ethic emerges from his own insight as a justified person. If Paul has an ethic, it is clear that it comes from some source other than outside authority. What we have been inspecting are only a few building blocks which he has lifted from other traditions and which he obviously uses because and only because they are consonant with *his own insights as a justified person.* Paul believes that he himself is competent to describe what the ethical acts of the justified person are to look like. After he has given the Corinthians the word of Jesus on divorce, he turns to another issue, mixed marriages, and intro-

duces the discussion by saying, "To the rest I say, not the Lord."
He has no command from Jesus about mixed marriages, but he
has no hesitancy in giving judgment. The interesting thing here
is that his permission of divorce in some extreme cases may be
actually a qualification of Jesus' logion which he has just cited.[6]
He does not apply the teaching of Jesus rigidly and actually feels
free to make exception or qualification if other considerations
seem to require it.

In the same discussion, but on another facet of the issue of
marriage, he says: "Now concerning the unmarried, I have no
command of the Lord, but I give my opinion as one who by the
Lord's mercy is trustworthy" (1 Cor. 7:25). And in the final case
in this sequence of instances, concerning the question of whether
a widow should remarry, Paul concludes, "But in my judgment
she is happier if she remains as she is. And I think that I have
the Spirit of God" (1 Cor. 7:40).

Now we would not be discussing Paul unless we were all in
agreement that he was a person of great spiritual insight. Indeed my own appreciation of him as a person who has plumbed
the depths of human existence is obvious. The question still
remains, Where does Paul get the confidence to make his own
judgments independently of consulting the oracles, whether of
the Scriptures, or of Jesus, or of Greek philosophy? Does it stem
out of his authority as Apostle to the Gentiles? Is Paul here
revealing himself as a domineering, commanding authority figure? Certainly Paul believed his call to be Apostle to the Gentiles was sacred and creative, and he had a strong sense of voca-
tional success—to use the term *vocation* in its proper religious
meaning. If he were simply domineeringly lording it over his
flock, however, he would be flaunting not only his theological
center but his basic ethical insights as well. And even if his
confidence stemmed from his sense of apostleship, it would say
nothing about the *content*.

Something more basic, something more linked with his theological center, is, I believe, at stake. My argument all along has

6. The issue depends upon whether the tradition about which Paul is knowledgeable included the words about divorce and remarriage (Mark 10: 10–12).
See the discussion in Dungan, *The Sayings of Jesus*, pp. 89–101, 132–33.

been that when persons live in faith before the God who gives life, they are restored to that creational nature which God had always intended for humanity, a nature which, according to Genesis 1, God affirmed to be "good." Because of this restoration persons are able, insofar as at any particular moment they live that faith, to use their faculties without the distortion which self-anxiety inevitably creates, without the repression of energy and function which is caused by the exhausting and exhaustive project of securing the self. Thus if it is part of that human nature intended by God for persons to love, they are now free to love. If it is part of that nature to be attuned noetically towards the neighbor, they are now free to see and hear with accuracy and caring perception. It is this caring perception which provides the insight into the being of others and into their needs, and which calls forth one's own being to meet those needs. And it is the freedom from fear, life now secure as gift, which gives one confidence to *try*, even in the face of obstacle and danger.

There is thus something *self-authenticating* about the life lived in faith. The believer, now restored to his or her created nature, experiences that "goodness" pronounced by God; and since it is that goodness basic to human existence, he or she is confident as never before that this life, this love, this knowledge is authentic and true. Thus, insofar and *only* insofar as the believer is living this faithful existence, he or she has a new caring perception and is confident in a new way that this perception is truer than all perceptions of the old existence.

If this is the case, why then did Paul use *any* material from the Old Testament, or Jesus, or Greek culture? If all is new, should not his ethic then be unique? The answer to this lies in his claim that a life in faith toward the God who justifies enables one to live an authentic *human* life. An ethic is to be judged not on whether it is unique, but on whether it is true, and Paul is certainly willing to hear the truth from whatever source. Although Christian existence is the noetic basis for understanding right action, the Apostle would hardly claim that only Christian believers have sensed the truth of authentic human action. Whether others can live that action is another matter and is not the issue here. Paul is thus free to look at whatever materials from whatever sources and choose from among them those state-ments, aphorisms, catalogues, and so on, which his transformed mind perceives to express the truth of authentic human living.[7]

Obviously such confidence skirts tremendous dangers. All people living enthusiastically within any system are liable to claim self-authentication, even within the systems of the worst demagogueries. People move inside and outside of their being, making noetic judgments all the while, without always being aware that their existential basis has moved and thus their per-ceptual base shifted. All people are tempted to escape their finiteness by confusing and identifying the caring perception with specific programs of assistance. Awareness of these dangers should not, however, be permitted to sabotage the basic confi-dence the believer has in his or her restoration by God's gift, although at the same time such persons need constantly to be sensitive to their own movement away from and back to the center of faithfulness. Is this what Jesus meant when he said, "Be innocent as doves and wise as serpents"?

Perhaps an example would be helpful at this point. I am in my office, anxiously trying to meet a deadline in my work. A student knocks at the door, enters, and asks if I have time to talk to him. Distracted by my work-pressure, still thinking of the work before me, I suggest he come back some other time. Per-haps he had some nonpressing matter after all; but suppose he was hurting, suppose he did very much need whatever counsel I could offer him just at that moment. My self-concern has blocked any perception I might have picked up of his hurt, any clues which his face or body may otherwise have communicated to me. Suppose on the other hand that, while I still have the same deadline, my sense of being is not at that moment anxious, threatened by the pressure of time. When the student enters, I ask him to sit down and I "listen" for clues as to his situation.

7. I do not doubt that there is essential agreement between Jesus and Paul. Before Paul, Jesus taught that life is a gift from God, although he taught in terms quite different from Paul (e.g., the parable of the prodigal son). The consonance and continuity between the two does not lie in the similarity of words or concepts but in that transformed reality which Jesus brought into being and which Paul participates in through the church. The Christian experience is the thread of continuity; the language used to describe that experience varies.

Perhaps, again, his visit is not important; then I could ask him to return later. But if he is hurting, I now have given him a chance to communicate that to me; my grounding in justification by grace at that moment frees me to be a neighbor to his need. After all, in most instances of ethical decision, what I *should* do is easily read from the situation, *if* I am free to know and care.

Thus I would suggest that both conduct and insight into conduct are part and parcel of that total existence of the eschatological person. Just as love spontaneously flows outward to others, so also insight as to how this love can best be harnessed and directed is inseparable from that total self of the eschatological person. If there is any truth to these reflections, then Paul's confidence and his ethical insights stem not from some demagoguery but from his own depth experience as a person justified by God's grace. A good tree produces not only good fruit, but good insights as well.

Two qualifications. First, this is no claim for Christian omniscience. We remain finite and faulty, and we continue to make mistakes in judgment. Nor is it a claim that Paul was himself omniscient. Few people would agree today with every ethical judgment Paul made—many, for example, have trouble with his rigidity on homosexuality. And it is obvious that Paul's world was vastly simpler than our own. Ethical judgments today about many matters cannot be adequately made without the consideration of complex scientific data. What I am suggesting is that the person justified by grace is pointed in a different direction and thus open to truer perceptions than before, but this is not to be taken as any educational shortcut. In fact, the new noetic perception makes the person aware that often scientific data *is* crucial to decision-making.

Secondly, Paul's ethical stance is close to a view in ethical discussion today called *situation ethics*. In this view there are no rules and regulations which predetermine a person's action. The concrete, unique situation of a person before the neighbor is itself an insight-producing situation and aids the person in directing appropriate action. Paul, it is true, has no rules and regulations. Paul also will listen to a concrete situation and have it inform him about proper action. And yet I am hesitant to pronounce Paul an outright "situationalist." In the first place

Paul, as we have yet to see, does provide guidelines, even if they are not rigid rules. In the second place, *more depends upon the quality of the existence of the ethical agent than upon the situation itself.* The situation will never tell us the right thing to do, as long as we are blinded by the project of securing our own existence and are therefore impotent to act for the other.

THE GUIDELINES

We are now ready to explore Paul's ethical wisdom, summed up in his guidelines. Although more guidelines could perhaps be suggested, I will list only four. The first three we have discussed before.

Freedom. The believer is freed *from* pietistic fears about physical contamination from objects and from all religious rules which separate the profane from the sacred. The believer is free *to* follow his or her own best judgments about actions, as long as these actions do not impinge upon the well-being of the other person.

There seems to be one important exception, in Paul's judgment, about such freedom, and that covers all aspects of sexuality. Paul can support sexual conduct only within the marriage bond. Sexual relations anywhere else are a serious offense: adultery, fornication, prostitution, and homosexuality.[8] The most serious issue here is not whether his judgments are faulty (although I do have problems with some of them) but whether he has adequately thought them through. His most strident, opaque, and logically inconsistent arguments tend to occur at points where the issue is either explicitly sexual or has implicit sexual overtones.

Peace. The security and reconciliation which is peace is another ethical guideline, as we have seen. It determines some of Paul's judgments about marriage and worship.

Love. We have already discussed the importance and quality of love in Paul's theology and ethics. Love as the fulfilling of the law is the key characteristic of relationship within the believing community.

---

8. For prostitution, see 1 Cor. 6:12–20; for the issue of women's dress and hair length (which at least indirectly bears on the question of sexuality) see 1 Cor. 11:2–16; for homosexuality, see Rom. 1:24–27, but cf. note 2 above.

The fourth guideline has to do with the question which then emerges, How does this love manifest itself, and what is the relation between love and freedom? Is there not a tension between them? Yes there is, but Paul is in no doubt here as to the proper resolution. For his key ethical guideline is what he calls the *upbuilding* of the neighbor, whether this upbuilding is directed toward the partner in marriage, the community in worship, or the brother at a dinner party. It should be instructive to see how this upbuilding works itself out in some of the day-to-day situations Paul addresses.

APPLICATIONS

The marriage bed. Here we return to 1 Corinthians 7, the discussion of various issues concerning marriage. The discussion itself marks a new beginning in the letter. Paul has had a number of questions put to him in a letter by the Corinthians, and now he turns to deal with them ("Now concerning the matters about which you wrote" [v. 1]). Although ancient Greek had no such thing as quotation marks, many scholars now think that the sentence that immediately follows is not Paul's own judgment but a quotation from the letter *by* the Corinthians, giving the view of some party within that church: "It is well for a man not to touch a woman." Paul then counters this view in the next sentence with his own judgment: "Because of the temptation to immorality, each man should have his own wife and each woman her own husband." Clearly we are here not simply within the sphere of marriage but within the specific sexual relation within marriage. Then follows what I think to be one of the most remarkable and succinct descriptions of marital sexual ethics in the history of the Christian tradition: "The husband should give to his wife her conjugal rights, and likewise the wife to her husband. For the wife does not rule over her own body, but the husband does; likewise the husband does not rule over his own body, but the wife does" (vv. 3-4).

Sexual ethics is here defined as one person giving his or her body for the pleasure of the other—and vice versa. Here both the *upbuilding* and the *mutuality* so characteristic of Paul's understanding of human relationships determine his judgments.

What is remarkable about this terse passage is that Paul is able to transcend the male-oriented, male-domineering understanding of sexuality which was a feature of his civilization (and which remains one of our own as well). The male is equally called to use his body to give pleasure to his wife. Whether male or female, one's body is offered to the other.

The dinner party. Again the Corinthians have asked him questions (1 Cor. 8:1-13; 10:23-31). We might reconstruct the question as, "How are we to reconcile the dispute amongst us about eating meat suspected of being previously sacrificed to pagan gods? Some of us say it's OK, since idols have no real existence, and we laugh at those weak brethren who are finicky about eating and who are worried that it might really be wrong and bring their salvation into question." Paul's response is clear, at least at the crucial points. Those who think it right to eat such meat are absolutely correct. One ought to be free to go to a dinner party given by a pagan friend and eat anything served without worry in one's conscience about anything. That is *freedom.*

But there is something more important than freedom—or I should say "someone"—and that is the brother or sister called "weak." "For if any one sees you, a man of knowledge, at table in an idol's temple, might he not be encouraged, if his conscience is weak, to eat food offered to idols? And so by your knowledge this weak man is destroyed, the brother for whom Christ died" (vv. 10–11). Just how Paul believed the weak person would be destroyed is not clear, at least to me, but the ethical principle is. "Therefore, if food is a cause of my brother's falling, I will never eat meat, lest I cause my brother to fall" (v. 13). The continual concern for the other overrules what otherwise would be a legitimate exercise of Christian freedom. The guideline of upbuilding takes precedence over that of freedom.

The worship service. Once more, the Corinthians. Even their worship services have become divisive (1 Cor. 12–14). Some people noisily speak in tongues and lord it over the less gifted who do not have that ability. Now we have already discussed the problem of pride involved with this free exercise of glossolalia. But there is another dimension. The communication of glossolalia is directly between a person and God. It is not directed to the brothers and sisters and does them no good. "For one who speaks in a tongue speaks not to men but to God; for no one understands him, but he utters mysteries in the Spirit. On the other hand, he who prophesies [that is, preaches] speaks to people for their upbuilding and encouragement and consolation. He who speaks in a tongue edifies himself, but he who prophesies edifies the church" (1 Cor. 14:2–4).

And there is the matter in a nutshell. Prophecy upbuilds the community while glossolalia does not. Therefore, speaking in tongues is not as important as prophecy. As if the issue were not already clear, Paul applies the decision to his own ministry. "I thank God that I speak in tongues more than you all; nevertheless, in church I would rather speak five words with my mind, in order to instruct others, than ten thousand words in a tongue" (1 Cor. 14:18–19).

With these little vignettes about things important but not earth-shattering—the everyday matters of sex in marriage, eating food, order in worship—Paul opens up the panorama of the total life of the justified person. In this life the person is free and yet constrained by love. One does not, however, give up the freedom with a petulant, "Well, if you insist." The person who truly lives life as gift probably never notices that he or she ever lost a moment of freedom. He or she is conscious only of that moment of love and finds true fulfillment in giving. In that giving there is, in fact, perfect freedom.

In his discussion in Romans of this same tension between freedom and love Paul sums it all up with an aphorism. Like any good aphorism it is not explained, and raises all sorts of questions. Yet, like a good aphorism, it encompasses a world. In this case it encompasses the world of faith and action, of justification and works, of the union of being and doing—in sum, it encompasses that world which is Paul's world of God's act in Christ for his creation. And I will no more try to explain it than does Paul himself. "For whatever does not proceed from faith is sin" (Rom. 14:23).

Epilogue

Many serious Christians are speaking about our present time as "post-Christian." They mean by this that any illusions that the church represents a majority culture in Europe or America are finally completely dissipated. The culture of the future can only be one of secular scientism. It is thus imperative to ask if there is any hope for a new day in the church and, from the perspective of our present discussion, whether Paul may be a part of that day.

Furthermore, the church does not seem to have a center about which it has confidence. It seems to be groping, almost in the dark, to find a place to stand which is a center of *faith* and yet which does not deny the modern age and the Christian's responsibility to it. The rapidly shifting movements in church thinking and acting in the last twenty years are indication enough of the tentativeness of the church's self-understanding.

The strong social protest of the church has collapsed; a potentially dangerous introversion has seized it. "How do I feel?" is a question that has replaced "What is the responsible thing to do?" The liberal churches and liberals within middle-road denominations, those who led the activist movement, are on the retreat; the conservative movement is growing in numbers and power. While conservatives still root their faith squarely in the Bible as the Word of God, most people in the more liberal part of the spectrum are, I think, perplexed about what to do with the Bible. At the other extreme, the secularists are reading it, when at all, as an interesting collection of ancient artifacts. One recent author symbolizes this direction through his article "The

Debut of the Bible as a Pagan Classic," suggesting that it be taught like the epics of Homer.[1] People are still trying to do theology, but most of the fledgling ventures in recent years have fluttered, too quickly exhausted, to the ground.

Thus few church leaders I know of are very confident about predicting what the future might be for the church. Some are not sure that it even has a future. I do not share the pessimism. While the church has no right to think that God will continue its existence no matter what it does, or doesn't, I do see signs of a continuing vitality precisely in the attempts being made to find a center. As long as the church, for all its finiteness and fallibility, struggles to assist God in his work in the world, I am confident it will continue to play a role in the history of God's world.

The conservative churches show clearly that our culture has not sold out to scientism and that the claim of the gospel can still be heard. The liberal churches also proclaim the gospel, even if they are not as certain about it as the conservative churches, and within that gospel is a challenge to make God's world a more humane place to live. Furthermore, the very fact that numerous attempts to do theology have been made in recent years indicates that many folk still believe theological reflection is, potentially at least, meaningful and important.

Equally significant, I believe, is the indication that Christians today are more willing to stand up for their beliefs without embarrassment and with a more open, less defensive posture. Three important theological-ethical statements have received attention in recent years in the United States. The first, the Chicago Declaration, was approved in 1973 by a group of conservative theologians, affirming the importance of the church's involvement in social action, precisely at a time when the liberal churches' push toward a better society was losing momentum.[2] Basing their stand upon the "Lord Jesus Christ and the full authority of the Word of God," they affirm that their biblical

1. J. Miles, Jr., in *The Bulletin of the Council on the Study of Religion*, vol. 7; No. 3 (June 1976).
2. R. Sider, ed., *The Chicago Declaration* (Carol Stream, Illinois: Creation House, 1974). This volume contains the declaration itself and a series of essays explaining and defending it.

faith necessitates an attack upon racism, sexism, materialism, and political and economic injustices.

The second, the Hartford Appeal, was drafted in 1975 by an ecumenical group of churchpeople from main-line denominations.[3] In it they attack what they feel is a dangerous Christian capitulation to secular relativism; they call the church and its theologians back to a sense of the transcendent God and the uniqueness of the Christian faith. "Salvation contains a promise of human fulfillment, but to identify salvation with human fulfillment can trivialize the promise. We affirm that salvation cannot be found apart from God." This appeal strives to nurture the *being* of the church.

The third and most recent statement, the Boston Affirmation, is motivated by the increasing quietism of the American churches, a fear of an irrelevant transcendence (which some people found expressed in the Hartford Appeal), and so calls for continued Christian concern for the improvement of the social order.[4] It is a strong statement of a theology of liberation. The transforming reality of God's reign is found, the statement emphasizes, in the struggles for liberation of the poor, the oppressed, racial minorities, and women from inhumane conditions. This appeal strives to nurture the *doing* of the church.

These are all healthy and ringing statements and are further indication of the continuing vitality of the church. They can be seen as attempts to find and hold to a center—although it is obvious that the center lies at a different point on the spectrum in each case. Thus they are also *warnings* against what they see as a movement by others away from the center. Some of the warnings can be stated as follows:

There is the warning against so falling into modern culture that the church sells out to *secular relativism*. Models from psychology and sociology may be so emphasized that the Chris-

3. The statement can now be found in *Against the World For the World: The Hartford Appeal and the Future of American Religion*, Peter L. Berger and Richard J. Neuhaus (New York: Seabury Press, 1976). This book also contains a series of essays about the intent of the statement.
4. The full text can be obtained from the Boston Industrial Mission, 56 Boylston Street, Cambridge, Massachusetts 02138.

tian faith is reduced to another way of speaking about human fulfillment. Thus Christianity becomes just one way among many of helping people toward realizing their potential. In this case, it is feared, the message of the gospel is relativized and secularized at the same time. The Hartford Appeal warns against this in its statement, "We affirm that salvation cannot be found apart from God." The warning is against denying a unique reality within the church.

A related warning to innovative theologians is to guard against losing contact with the basic theological statements of the Bible and the historic church. From the standpoint of those who see the Bible as the primary source of revelation, recent "theologies of" or "theologies and" are suspect.[5] Unless theology is rooted in the proclamation found in Scripture it may also be a sell-out to secularism. When psychology, sociology, and various forms of philosophy determine the language and content of theology, in what sense can it still be considered *Christian* theology?

There is the warning of the Hartford Appeal that the world should not set the agenda for the church. It sets itself against the proposition that "social, political and economic programs to improve the quality of life are ultimately normative for the church's mission in the world." By this it seems to wish to assert, without denying the importance of social action, that there is something more to the mission of the church than for it simply to be one among a number of social agencies.

But the warnings move in the opposite direction as well. The Boston Affirmation responds to the Hartford Appeal by finding "the transforming reality of God's reign" precisely in those secular and religious attempts to remove injustice and improve the lives of people. Without this awareness and concern the framers of this statement are fearful that the church becomes "transmuted into a club for self- or transcendental awareness." That is, they warn against seeing the church become only the place where an *irrelevant transcendence* is worshiped and the needs of the world thus left unheard and ignored.

---

5. Such as theology of the death of God, theology of revolution, theology of sexuality, theology and psychology, theology and sociology, theology and literature.

A related warning against a church which attends to its own existence and sees itself as somehow unique is that against elitism. If salvation is only in the church, are not church members better, or at least better off? The world is here too neatly divided between the saved and the damned, and it is too easy for the church to consider itself a community of individuals superior to all others.

Surely in all of this there is a continuous struggle to find a center, a place to stand where the gospel in all its ramifications and implications can be most completely expressed. We need in the church today a place, a perspective which can be inclusive rather than exclusive, that can say *both/and* rather than *either/or—without watering down either of the realities being held in tension.* In short, we need a theology where the tensions of being and doing are held together creatively and in some ultimate union.

In this book I have tried to argue that Paul's theological reflections provide us with just such a center where being and doing cannot be separated and where neither is minimized at the expense of the other. I have tried to show that the faith stance described by Paul as "justification by grace through faith" provides us a profound grounding which can inform both contemporary theological reflection and contemporary ethical action. This is obviously not to say that we can just repeat Paul's words and that no other theological thinking is necessary. It is a truism that theology must be rethought and rewritten for each generation. We may not even choose to continue the specific vocabulary of Paul's mythological system (although I see no inherent problems in keeping it, if we know what he means by it). But it is a claim that that basic Christian *reality* before the gracious God, which Paul describes so well, must be the basis for whatever we think and do as Christian believers.

For Paul, being and doing are the single unity of the person justified by God-in-Christ. Thus, on the one hand, Paul celebrates the salvational realities within the community of faith. Joy, peace, freedom, mutual love, an expressive emotional and intellectual life of authentic persons—all these are central to the reality of a church living under justification by grace. There *is* (or should be) a reality within the church not found in the secular world. Furthermore, it is a communal life, thus overcoming the isolated individualism of so much Christianity. There is no personal salvation that is not consummated within the mutuality of the believing community.

On the other hand, *doing* is equally a part of that salvational reality. It is, first, the doing of love and care for the fellowship of believers. But I believe it is also the doing in the world outside, in that old, demonic world where indifference and brutality harm and kill. Paul has no program of social gospel in his letters, yet he does believe that God-in-Christ is lord of the entire cosmos, and Paul points all believers, if only implicitly, to that world. And since salvation for Paul engages the total person, the mission to the world also engages those forces which affect the total selfhood of others, material as well as spiritual. Were Paul alive with us today, I believe he would affirm, with the Chicago Declaration, that "God lays total claim upon the lives of all his people. We cannot, therefore, separate our lives in Christ from the situation in which God has placed us in the United States and the world."

Paul's theology also lays to rest any danger of elitism within the church. In fact, it plainly destroys it, at the same time without denying the new and realized life within the community. Justification by grace does create new persons; but the new self can only continue to exist as long as it acknowledges that the new is sheer gift. Since an elitist position is actually based on justification by works (I am better than you because of what *I* am or what I *do*), it is diametrically opposite to that new life which lives in justification by grace. Thus any believer who claims to be a member of the elite denies by that very claim any rootage in justification by grace and thus in the new life itself as Paul understood it. This is in effect what Paul says to the Corinthians (1 Cor. 1–4). No believer can boast save in the Lord. No believer can exult either over other believers or over nonbelievers. Paul, as we have seen, refuses to pass judgments on those outside the community of faith.

Perhaps even more needs to be said. God's act in Christ is an act for the entire world, and Paul's theology of the new creation points to the universalism of that act. The church is important only because it is there that the new creation exists. Thus a proper statement of the relation is not, "Wherever the church is, there is the new creation," but rather, "Wherever the new creation is, there is the church." The church remains the servant of the new creation.

The question then becomes whether the new creation exists outside of the explicit walls of the church. Paul himself never raised the question, but his theology of the new creation does, I believe, point in that direction. God has acted for the *world*, with the church as servant. Now if the world is the primary object rather than the church, then the correct implication from that position is surely that God is free to act with his world as he chooses, even if Paul never made an explicit statement to that effect. The posture of new life is *always* to be seen as the living out of the sense that life is gift. How a person understands and verbalizes that posture may, however, vary.

This affirmation still makes God the source of salvation. Thus we can be free to celebrate the new creation wherever it exists, within the church or without, and still claim that "salvation cannot be found apart from God."

If we choose to stand with Paul, we can, furthermore, affirm both that salvation is a restoration to authentic creatureliness and at the same time that the source of salvation lies in God's act in Christ. Salvation can thus be described in secular, humanistic terms, using whatever models are appropriate, without denying that "salvation cannot be found apart from God."

Finally, standing with Paul gives us a *theology rooted in the biblical witness*. I have tried to show that this theology is not an abstract mythology but a meaning-structure deeply rooted in the transformation of persons in God's act in Christ. Such a theology would enable a common language to be spoken and understood across the theological spectrum. There will always be differences between conservative and liberal on the place of the Bible. For myself, I do not believe Paul because he is in some a priori way authoritative. I consider him authoritative because I believe him, that is, because he speaks to me and gives me at least a vision which I can on occasion experience of the transforming power of God's act in Christ. My conservative colleagues would put it the other way around. Yet even they acknowledge the inner witness of the Holy Spirit and should thus understand and appreciate what I say. For all the differences, however, through Paul we could speak from a biblical basis and communicate crucial matters of faith and theology through this common language.

Will there be a new day for the church? I can only hope, and I hope with passion that when it comes Paul will be a part of that new day. For while there are many other ways of stating the gospel message, I do believe that he has found a way of expressing the very depths of God's liberating and redeeming act as it touches the present lives of people like you and me. Paul is there for us in that new day, if we dare to live in faith before the God who graciously gives us new life. May that new day be today for the church.

Index of Scriptural Passages